BY THE SAME AUTHOR

Unscientific Americans; Parallel Universes; Mondo Boxo;
The Four Elements; Proof of Life on Earth; Childproof;
and The Party, After You Left.

THEORIES OF EVERYTHING

SELECTED, COLLECTED, AND HEALTH-INSPECTED CARTOONS, 1978-2006

$$X = \frac{2}{3}m + \left\{\pi \frac{17}{32}\right\}' \div \square^2 + \frac{xyz}{abc}(a^2+b^2+c^2) - 5\left(\frac{Y}{X}\right)^2 \div \left\{\frac{x(m)}{Y(m^2)}\right\} + \quad / \frac{abc}{\odot} + m\left(\frac{xy}{yx}\right)$$

ROZ CHAST

BLOOMSBURY

To my parents,
Elizabeth and George

All right, already.

<u>Theories of Everything</u> collects the best of Roz Chast's cartoons from the last twenty-nine years. They originally appeared in the periodicals *Double Take*, *House & Garden*, *The New Yorker*, *Redbook*, *The Sciences*, *Scientific American*, and *Worth*, and the books *Unscientific Americans*, *Parallel Universes*, *Mondo Boxo*, *The Four Elements*, *Proof of Life on Earth*, *Childproof*, and *The Party, After You Left*.

 Copyright © 2006 by Roz Chast
Introduction © 2006 by David Remnick

Published by Bloomsbury Publishing, New York and London
Distributed to the trade by Holtzbrinck Publishers

All papers used by Bloomsbury Publishing are natural, recyclable products made from wood grown in well-managed forests. The manufacturing processes conform to the environmental regulations of the country of origin.

Library of Congress Cataloging-in-Publication Data has been applied for.

ISBN-13:978-1-58234-423-2/ISBN-10:1-58234-423-X (hardback edition)
ISBN-13:978-1-59691-320-2/ISBN-10:1-59691-320-7 (paperback edition)

First U.S. Edition 2006
3 5 7 9 10 8 6 4 2

Printed and bound in the United States of America by Worzalla

LITTLE THINGS

I'm not saying that Roz Chast lives with more domestic anxiety than the rest of us, but I am compelled to report that the first time I saw her at *The New Yorker*'s old offices on West Forty-third Street her son, Ian, was standing next to her juggling a set of carving knives. The ceiling was low, the blades sharp, but that boy had remarkably fast hands for an eleven-year-old, you had to give him that. Years later, when I asked Roz why Ian juggled knives, she said, "I think he does it to relax. And to scare me."

Like everyone who works at the magazine and everyone who reads it, I loved her distinctive cartoons—but before the Day of the Flying Daggers I'd never laid eyes on her, only on her sublime drawings. But as I brought the picture into focus—that is, when I put on my glasses and looked down the hall more carefully at this smallish woman with her large horn-rims, her expression of wised-up anxiety—it seemed obvious: The visitor was "that woman from the Roz Chast cartoons." I'd have known her on the street or on the subway; I'd have known her anywhere. The fact that her son was doing a pretty good imitation of Eddie Munster only made it a little easier to figure out.

If you read, and live in, this extraordinary book for a while, you'll see (not to be over-fancy about it) that these drawings are as personal and direct as any writer's diaries. Pepys was withholding by comparison. All of Roz Chast's anxieties, fears, superstitions, failures, furies, insecurities, and dark imaginings—all of it, the entire kit and caboodle of her psyche, is here, and you feel that you are meeting a vivid, deep, funny, peculiar, and *particular* human being. All of the best cartoonists, and all of Chast's favorites—William Steig, Saul Steinberg, Gahan Wilson, Sam Gross, Jack Ziegler, Helen Hokinson, Otto Soglow, Bruce Eric Kaplan, and Mary Petty of *The New Yorker*, as well as Winsor McCay, Harvey Pekar, Robert Crumb, Don Martin, Edward Gorey, and Ernie Bushmiller (to name a very few)—defy the conventions of what is funny and reflect a distinctive inner life.

"When a cartoon makes me laugh, or when anything makes me laugh, to me it's magic," Roz once wrote. "It's circumvented the My Life Is a Serious Business, and How Can We Laugh When People Are Starving (or Eating a Fast-Food Diet and Becoming Morbidly Obese) circuit. Which is, like, a miracle." Her unmistakable drawings, with their crumbly yet accurate lines, are perfect for what she's doing, a natural extension of the persona and her voice. "This is just the way I draw; it's how I've always drawn," she's said. "I think of it like handwriting."

What also makes Roz great is that it *seems* that what she does must be sort of easy. There are those, too, who must also think that it's easy for John Updike to throw the voice of Henry Bech or Harry Angstrom, for Woody Allen to project Fielding Mellish and Miles Monroe. No such luck. We've all got anxieties and domestic secrets, but Roz Chast has the genius of comic invention to make them funny. To memorialize her sense of maternal inadequacy, for example, she invented a drawing of "Bad Mom" trading cards. (Mom No. 89: "While on the phone, told child to SHUT THE HELL UP or she would brain her.") Everything that passes before her daily life—unruly kids; aging parents baffled by modern technology; the miscommunication in a mixed marriage; negotiating the suburbs with a poor grasp of driving and a lousy sense of direction; anxieties about having forgotten every piece of knowledge from the eighth grade on—it's all fodder for her ongoing, comic self-examination.

Roz Chast grew up in an unfancy part of Brooklyn. Her parents were schoolteachers. When I turned forty, some friends and colleagues bought for me what is my most prized possession—an autobiographical strip of hers that describes how her parents used to take her upstate to Cornell in the summertime for "a certain degree of intellectualism." In just a few panels we get a portrait of the artist as a young girl. While her parents went off to their lectures and courses, they'd leave Roz behind at a library on the Cornell campus where she spent hours reading cartoon books by Peter Arno, George Price, and, especially, her favorite, the extravagantly creepy Charles Addams, author of *Monster Rally*, *Black Maria*, *Nightcrawlers*, and *Drawn and Quartered*.

The Roz character in the strip recalls, "I laughed at everything that I knew I shouldn't find funny: homicidal spouses; kids building guillotines in their rooms; and all those poor, unfortunate two-headed, three-legged, four-armed people. Wolcott Gibbs, in his introduction to *Addams and Evil*, wrote that Addams's work 'is essentially a denial of all spiritual and physical evolution in the human race.' All in all, I'd have to agree."

Roz sold her first cartoon to *The New Yorker* in 1978. She was certainly not an imitator of the gothic Addams style—she didn't really imitate anyone—but she had not yet invented her comic self. And yet she was already an innovator. The drawing is called "Little Things" and it shows a collection of nonsense shapes—are they miniature tools? ill-formed beer nuts?—that go by neologisms that *seem* to be English words: "chent," "enker," "redge," and so on. William Shawn, who edited the magazine for thirty-five years, rightly earned a measure of fame for having brought countless writers to public attention; he also deserves credit for seeing the virtue of "chent," "enker," and "redge," and the emerging talent of Roz Chast. Back then (and to this day), even the wildest imaginations among the cartoonists almost always kept within the frame and conventions of the gag cartoon. Roz is always creating something different: fake greeting cards, a triptych of fake Sylvia Plath poems, a three-page strip in the form of a family car vacation. She has published nearly a thousand drawings in *The New Yorker* and has never fallen into set patterns. If the magazine employs an artistic genius since the passing of Saul Steinberg and William Steig, Roz Chast is the one.

Not long ago, I called Roz at her house in Connecticut and we had an anxiety-and-silence-free conversation—until I slipped in one of those where-do-you-get-your-ideas questions. I'm afraid that you, dear reader, are going to have to enjoy this book and this sublime artist without the benefit of an edifying answer, because, as best as I can remember, what she said was "Oh God, this is about the moment when I hang up on you."

—DAVID REMNICK

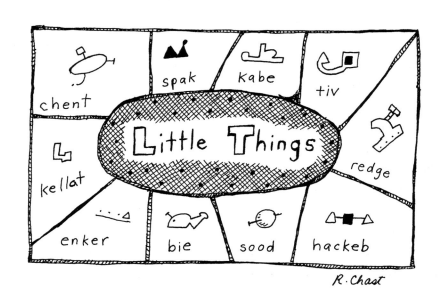

TUESDAY NIGHT FEVER

R. Chast

FALSE STARTS

 It all began with a shoe,

 and a cup and saucer

 It all began with a shoe,

 and the three Jones children,

 It began with an old book with a green cover.

 A red cover.

Roz Chast

ROZ CHAST

remains of

ANCIENT SUBURBIA

(mid 20th c.)

Bust of woman
Found near New Rochelle, N.Y.

Some Household Items,
Hasbrouck Heights, N.J.

Ceremonial Garb,
Babylon. L.I.

Roz Chast

Artificial Fruit of
Syosset, L.I.

RUDENESS GALORE

R. Chast

Vegetable Musicale

Roz Chast

ROZ CHAST

OUR FRIEND ALGEBRA

Let A = Joe	Let B = Moe
Let c = Flo	Let D = Spo

R. Chast

BOUND for BROADWAY

Ta da da da

Da ta da ta

Better get rid of these brown shoes.

R. Chast

ROZ CHAST

Dear Alicia,

I am just having TONS of FUN here at the Sunnyside Hotel.

I am with Mom and Dad and Fritz. Fritz had a stomach-ache from eating some weird potato chips.

We went to the beach. I found three shells.

I met this girl She is a creep. She is in this hotel.

He is better now.

We had fried fish pieces for dinner last night. Then we watched TV in the hotel room.

 (assortment)

So long. I'm really having the time of my life.

Jill

R. Chast

SOME POSSIBLE ANSWERS

Drain the Hudson; move everybody to Montana.

Require people to spend one day a week inside.

Massive, modern superstructures just like this one.

A nice, tall glass of water with no ice in it.

Methodical, neat arrangement of everything

R. Chast

Heartbreak Hotel

 There isn't any hot water.

 They charge $3.00 for one slice of burnt toast.

 The bellhop is surly.

R. Chast

You can dress them up, but you can't take them out.

R. Chast

AVERAGE JOES

Joe Stone

Joe Parker

Joe McGillicuddy

Joe $\sqrt{7999k}$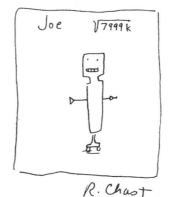

R. Chast

UNCOMMON STILL-LIFES

Tomato, Glass of Water, and Toast

Book and Cleaning Product

Chicken Leg and Vase

Chips and Dip on Oilcloth

R. Chast

ROZ CHAST

THE REJECTS

ROZ CHAST

TOO CUTE FOR COMFORT

Here They Are

VARIOUS HIGHWAY LIGHTS
and their nicknames

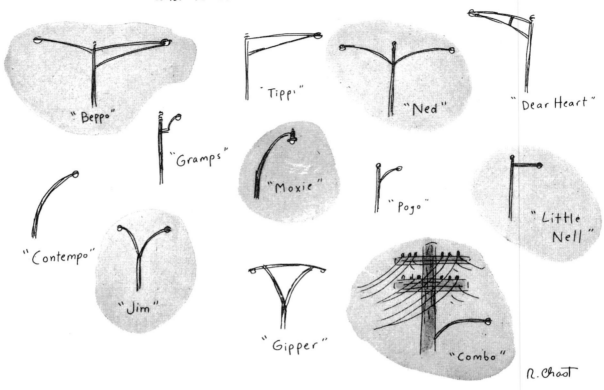

"Beppo"

"Tipp"

"Ned"

"Dear Heart"

"Gramps"

"Moxie"

"Pogo"

"Little Nell"

"Contempo"

"Jim"

"Gipper"

"Combo"

R. Chast

MUSTS TO AVOID

This store.

ACME CLOTHES CORP.

This product.

N²

This philosophy.

Life is like a bucket of oats.

R. Chast

ROZ CHAST

THE FOUR MAJOR FOOD GROUPS

Regular:

Hamburger, cola, French fries,
fruit pie.

Company:

Cracker variety, canapé,
"interesting" cheese, mint.

Remorse:

Plain yogurt, soybeans,
mineral water, tofu.

Silly:

Space-food sticks, gelatine mold
with fruit salad in it,
grasshopper pie.

R. Chast

The Guided Tour

R. Chast

EN ROUTE

R. Chast

STRANGE PROVERBS

The ketchup of sorrow
is better than
the mustard of happiness.

Three shoes do not
a hat make.

A couch is as
good as a chair.

A song in time is
worth a dime.

Hop before
you skip.

R. Chast

The Miniature Sports

Miniature tennis

Miniature baseball

Miniature swimming

R. Chast

ROZ CHAST

YOUTH WANTS TO KNOW

Why did Lucinda dye her hair?

R. Chast

Why did Billy throw out this book?

LIFE'S HAT

Why did Sheila cancel her subscription to "Entity"?

ENTITY

Why did Richard sell his shell collection?

FOODS OF THE DEMIGODS

Raisin toast

Cheese omelette

Shells

MACARONI
797326

R. Chast

RAPTURES

R. Chast

LAUNDRY TRIPTYCH

ROZ CHAST

WEDNESDAYS on JUPITER

Kinda short!

Kinda cold!

Kinda big!

All in all, kinda neat!

R. Chast

CAT'S PAJAMAS

(comes with a hat)

R. Chast

The Three Certainties

DEATH

TAXES

BOBO

R. Chast

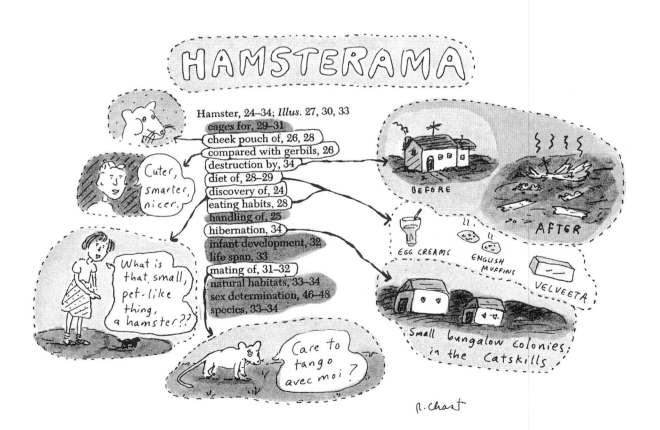

HAMSTERAMA

Hamster, 24–34; *Illus.* 27, 30, 33
cages for, 29–31
cheek pouch of, 26, 28
compared with gerbils, 26
destruction by, 34
diet of, 28–29
discovery of, 24
eating habits, 28
handling of, 25
hibernation, 34
infant development, 32
life span, 33
mating of, 31–32
natural habitats, 33–34
sex determination, 46–48
species, 33–34

Cuter, smarter, nicer.

What is that small, pet-like thing, a hamster??

Care to tango avec moi?

BEFORE

AFTER

EGG CREAMS

ENGLISH MUFFINS

VELVEETA

Small bungalow colonies in the Catskills

R. Chast

ROZ CHAST

LITTLE BEVERLY CARDS

SAVE 'EM • COLLECT 'EM • TRADE 'EM

#792
Little Beverly stares off into space.

#876
Little Beverly contemplates getting a cold.

#1101
Little Beverly experiences free-floating anxiety.

R. Chast

INCONSPICUOUS CONSUMPTION

The smallest tube of toothpaste.

NEON

A new ironing-board cover.

Three boxes of cereal.

R. Chast

THURSDAY, 1 A.M.

NEVER THE EXPERIMENT

ALWAYS THE CONTROL

ROZ CHAST

THE LADY OR THE TIGER OR THE CLOSET?

R. Chast

HELL'S BELLS

R. Chast

THE GIRL WITH THE SENSIBLE SHOES

PLINYS

NANOOK GOES SOUTH

Sick of the North, Nanook heads for Florida.

He is shocked to discover the unavailability of blubber, his favorite snack.

He is boiling in his parka, but old habits die hard.

R. Chast

PROSPERITY IS...

A) Across the street?

B) Over the river and through the woods?

C) Under the boardwalk?

D) Around the corner, down two blocks, a little to the left, about ½ a mile past a large intersection, etc.?

YOU ARE HERE

R. Chast

The Cereal's Universe

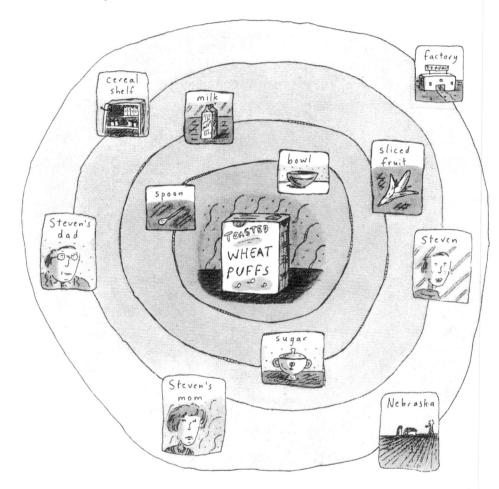

THE AGE OF REASONS

NO VACANCIES

COUSINS GO CRAZY

The night all the cousins stayed in one room, things got a little out of hand.

It all began with the customary joke-telling

What's green and skates?

Aunt Rose came in and told us to quiet down and go to sleep.

Hey, kids! Pipe down! Go to sleep!

This only made the jokes seem funnier.

HO HO HEE HEE HA

We pushed all the beds & cots together in the middle of the room—

and made ourselves a trampoline

We thought it wouldn't be quite as noisy.

What are you kids doing??

About 20 minutes later, we started taking all the foam rubber pillows out of their cases & shredding them.

That's when the lights went on.

R. Chast

ROZ CHAST

SIGNS OF CIVILIZATION

Coasters.

Matching towels.

Checkbook holders with sayings on them.

GONE WITH THE WIND

Automatically opening address books.

addresses

R. Chast

NOT THE BEST POLICY

1/17/84

Dear Aunt Mary,
   Too bad you sent me that hideous sweater. I hardly know what to do with it.

Ungratefully,
Susan

1/23/84

Dear Mary.
   Why'd you send me a tie? I have so many already.

Disappointedly,
Jim

JAN. 15

DEAR AUNTY,
YOUR CHEESY TOYS ALWKYS BREAK 2 SECONDS AFTER I GET THEM.

BITTERLY,
TIMMY

R. Chast

THEORIES OF EVERYTHING

The ALARMIST'S CORNER

Today is Thursday.

Uh oh!

A few days ago, it was Sunday.

Oh, no!

There are seven days in a week.

What are we going to do???

Dumbo's Distant Cousins

BIMBO

RUMBO

MAMBO

DIMBO

RAMBO

FIRST NOSTALGIA

There was a snap in the air, 	and we thought we could detect a faint scent of coffee candies, 	the kind Grandma always had around. 
It was getting dark earlier and earlier. 	Were Christmas decorations going up already? 	We had to pick up some items at the store for Mom. 
When we got out, night had almost fallen upon the city. 	We detoured through the park, 	but we had to hurry because dinner was always at six. 
We saw this neat dog. 	There was the smell of winter! 	That's when we got nostalgic. 

R. Chast

FIVE LITTLE TINIES at home...

Bill
Tim
Marsha
sue
Ed

What are you watching, Ed?

"A Tiny Christmas"– it was made in 1939

It's not bad... what are you cooking? Smells good.

It's your favorite: BREAD-CRUMB SURPRISE.

We'll be eating bread-crumb for weeks!!!

© R. Chast 78

POSTCAMBRIAN ANTICS

It was one of those days.

A baby laughed, a fuse blew,

HA HA HO HO

Darn it.

people stopped thinking about politics;

I'll take it!

and somewhere, a container of milk "turned."

R. Chast

ROZ CHAST

NEW MOVIE GENRES

Sci-fi/Western

Musical/Self-help

Sports/Horror

Documentary/Romance

NIGHT DRIVE

Well, it really all began with a car trip we took one night in May...

There was me and Tim and Jane, with Tim driving.

Somehow we wound up on route 84.

Around 10 PM we stopped at a LUK-EE DONUT place for some refreshment.

At first we were going to "take-out" but we changed our minds upon entering the establishment.

The abundance of pinks in the room was enough to make us stay awhile.

We ordered 3 coffees, 2 whole wheat honey glazed donuts and a jelly roll donut.

Tim smoked a Kool.

Once more we were on our way. On the car radio we got a station from Wheeling, West Virginia.

There was really quite alot of static, but for a while it was interesting.

We even heard a really hilarious news bulletin about a UFO sighting...

At about 12:30 AM, we pulled into the lot of a huge all-night supermarket where people bought in BULK.

ROZ CHAST

We thought we'd give it a whirl and pick up some stuff.

We needed some juice, bread, cheese, cookies, and magazines. The place was really merchandiseville.

We couldn't find anything that we needed, so we got some bottled water and organic chips.

We bought some crackers and aerosol cheese just for entertainment.

THINGS YOU CAN DO:

Now we felt seriously on our way. Jane fell asleep.

When she awoke she told us her dream. "We were all in Nice, staying at the Negresco."

It was slightly boring, but we didn't really mind.

Then you said, where's my Vodka Collins, etc.

Shortly after that, we passed some projects... It was around 2 AM by then, but we were pretty "up."

I remember thinking that I was having the time of my life, but I don't know why.

We had drifted away from WWVA and were now onto some station with a lot of homemade commercials.

CUMMON DOWN TO ED'S and he'll treat you like a KING!

We talked about: our favorite styles of clothing; Chinese food; people we knew in common; our adolescences; our parents; ice cream; very small towns; and public transportation.

The sun began to come up, and suddenly everything felt different.

R. Chast

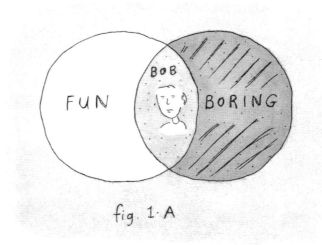

fig. 1·A

R. Chast

The Tabletop Family

They make their home on a tabletop,
where fun and laughter never stop.
They're smart and nice and very cute,
much better than a bowl of fruit.

R. Chast

ROZ CHAST

PARALLEL UNIVERSES

OURS:
It's 4:27 P.M., and Mrs. N. is baking cookies.

UNIVERSE #78332986 01:
It's 203:97 ZFK, and Mrs. Vvv. is baking pilkers.

UNIVERSE #80355476:
It's $\frac{109}{L}$, and Trr is baking sppooo.

UNIVERSE #$\sqrt{B}$:
It's $\oint_E$, and $\&$ is

*"I'll make a deal with you. You don't push my buttons,
and I won't pull your strings."*

Superheroes

Stands up to the wear and tear of everyday life!

Doesn't let little things get to him!

Still likes people even after living in New York for several years!

ROZ CHAST

FROM BAD TO WORSE

Plastic rainhats.

Plastic rainhats that fold up in packets.

Plastic rainhats in packets that have a bank's name on them.

SHADY SAVINGS BANK AND LOAN

Aforementioned item given as a "gift" to someone

I'd like you to have this!

?

R. Chast

PLANET OF THE GUYS

FAVORITE
WATER DRINKS

H₂O Punch

2 c. tap water

2 c. well water

1 c. bottled spring water

1 c. distilled water

Place ingredients in blender. Mix well.

Serves 6-8.

Alaska

Place 1 qt. water* in refrigerator for 2-4 hours. Serve immediately.

Makes 4 portions.

* any kind

Water Spritzer

Pour 2 oz. of distilled or bottled spring water in a glass over ice. Fill with club soda.

Make Mine Water

1 c. tap water

Decorate with tiny umbrella. Serves 1.

R Chast

THE MAN WHO DARED TO LEAVE HIS JOB
RIGHT IN THE MIDDLE OF THE DAY
JUST TO GO HOME AND TAKE A HOT BATH!!!!

CRUISES TO NOWHERE

THE CAR

THE FAMILY

ATTACK OF THE

YOUNG PROFESSIONALS!

Watch in horror as they...

...turn your neighborhood into an overpriced, high-rent boutiqueland!

...talk about their investments right in front of your eyes!

Merrill Lynch says oxen, mung beans, and rare keychains.

...dress for success even while sleeping!

WRONG   RIGHT

ROZ CHAST

RECIPES
from the
AMERICAN CHEESE COUNCIL

Cheese Omelette

2 eggs
5 lb. Swiss cheese
1 tbsp. butter

Melt butter in pan. Add eggs and cheese. Cook until done. Serves 2.

Cheese Salad

1 tomato	1 lb. feta cheese
1 mushroom	1 lb. blue cheese
1 leaf of lettuce	1 lb. Parmesan
2 lb. cheddar	½ lb. Camembert
1 lb. Muenster	½ lb. Gruyère

Make everything bite-sized, then place in bowl. Serves 6 cheese-loving people.

Cheese Patties

6 lb. soft cheese

Form cheese into patties. Serve on a bun. Makes enough for 12 patties.

Cheese Pick-Me-Up

½ cup water
1 lb. Brie

Put everything in blender at a high speed. Serve immediately. Just enough for one.

r. Chast

ROZ CHAST

CAB FROM HELL

IN A QUANDARY

"STAR WARS:" THE FINAL INSTALLMENT

Everyone in "Star Wars" and everyone in "Star Trek" winds up being related,

UNCLE KIRK!!!

except for Princess Leia, who is ultimately revealed to be an android.

In the very last scene, it all turns out to be some kid's nightmare.

R. Chast

THE YOUNG
JACQUES COUSTEAU
AT THE BEACH
WITH HIS MOTHER

Regardez!

R. Chast

ROZ CHAST

MOMS of OTHER PLANETS

THE VELCROS AT HOME

ROZ CHAST

EARN DOLLARS A DAY BY
DOING ABSOLUTELY NOTHING!

HERE'S HOW!

You just sit in your favorite chair! When an hour's up,
we pay you $10.00! Just like that!!

There has to
be a catch!

Tick,
tick, tick!

BUT THERE'S
NO CATCH!!!

To find out more, write to:

BUCKS GIVEAWAY
23 UNBELIEVABLE ST.
WOW, MONTANA

R. Chast

TOPIC PROCESSOR

PERFECT MASTERS

FIGHT IT OUT

Who has the most Rolls-Royces? The cutest disciples? The longest beard? The nicest swimming pool? The best lawyers? The biggest landholdings? The spiffiest outfit?

LITE® BOOKS

Madame Bovary LITE®

Madame B., dissatisfied with her lot in life, goes on a shopping spree. Later, she returns everything but a hat.

Anna Karenina LITE®

Anna K., a married woman, has a date with a Count Vronsky. He moves away, and they never see each other again.

Crime and Punishment LITE®

Raskolnikov writes a nasty letter to a pawn-broker, but later feels guilty and apologizes.

ROZ CHAST

EVEN AS A CHILD, HE PREFERRED TO RIDE THE
LITTLE COUCH AREA
OF THE MERRY-GO-ROUND.

HYPOCHONDRIA
CARDS

4 HYPO-ALLERGENIC CARDS IN EACH HERMETICALLY SEALED PACKET, PLUS 1 STICK VERY ORGANIC GUM

#93- BENGALI FOOT FEVER ~

Foot itches; cough; mood change.

#104 - GEEBLER'S SYNDROME ~

Queasiness; hands feel overly warm.

#216 - TURVEY'S DISEASE ~

Strange taste in mouth; joints ache.

#275 - HARNIK'S CONDITION ~

Memory lapse; arm hurts when pinched a certain way.

R. Chast

The Imperfect Hostess

R. Chast

R. Chast

LIFE GETS LUSH

R. Chast

THE CRAZY HOUR

Face gets wild.

Back hunches up. ("Halloween kitty")

Noisy runs after invisible things.
GALUMPH GALUMPH

Back to normal.

R. Chast

RALPH NADER'S CHILDREN

We just like to buy and buy and buy.

So what if things break?

Then you get to go out and buy some new ones!

R. Chast

BAD TRANSLATION

Peter Pan, what is?

Is pan with personality what flies around.

Is little pan with not grow up desire feeling.

NOT WANT TO GO TO SCHOOL

Is likened by children.

The Peter Pan is friend.

R. Chast

TINY CLAIMS COURT

Neighbor's dog chewed pencil.

Flapjack mix from Dalemart bought by N.M. was spoiled.

E-Z BATTER
Flapjack
A

While sewing at T.F.'s house, claimant pricked self with borrowed needle.

R. Chast

Aug. 4, 1986   THE NEW YORKER   Price $1.50

ROZ CHAST

SEASONS AND THEIR BUDGETS

SPRING: New leaves;
birds; flowers; rain;
grass ~
$286,938,557,651,921,000.⁰⁰

FALL: Dyes for leaves ~
$109,692,280,553,281,000.⁰⁰

WINTER: Snow ~
$878,652,339,102,000.⁰⁰

SUMMER: More rain;
grass; leaves ~
$486,229,357,293,000.⁰⁰

R. Chast

ROGUE SALAD BAR

KEYS PENNIES POCKET LINT STAMPS OIL VINEGAR

SHOELACES TISSUES OLD NEGATIVES BUTTONS BOBBY PINS CHECKERS

R. Chast

SINGIN IN THE RAIN

THE END OF INNOCENCE

ROZ CHAST

CUTIFICATION

It was only a matter of time before cutification hit our neighborhood.

The first sign of the coming cuteness was what happened to Al's Shoe Repair.

AL'S SHOO-BE-DO

FREE BALLOONS!

C'MON IN

There was nothing anyone could do about it, either.

Within six months, either you were cute or you were gone.

THE DRY CLEANING BOUTIQUE-CAFÉ

R. Chast

FAILURES

Pavlov's cat

DING DING DING

?

Pavlov's bird

?

CLANG

Pavlov's plant

BING BONG

?

R. Chast

HUMPTY-DUMPTY

More Hamptons

Tubhampton

Fanhampton

Roofhampton
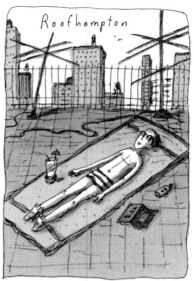

R. Chast

LLOYD:

A MAN WHO WOULDN'T KNOW A GOOD TIME IF IT HIT HIM ON THE HEAD, KNOCKED HIM OUT COLD, TIED HIS HANDS AND FEET, AND LEFT HIM IN A LITTLE TOOL SHED TO PERISH.

R. Chast

ROZ CHAST

SELECTIONS FROM

THE SLICED PEACH COLLECTION

OF SHELLEY B.

Happy Sliced Peaches
Briartree, Minnesota
October 15, 1961

Verigood Sliced Peaches
Sheldon, Wisconsin
February 8, 1963

Ambrosia Sliced Peaches
Surplus City, Nebraska
September 20, 1964

Jumpin' Jehosephat
Sliced Peaches
Mildwood, Kentucky
May 12, 1968

Wepackum Sliced
Peaches
Lake Veal, Iowa
March 17, 1970

Honey Sliced Peaches
Huldro Corners, Illinois
November 5, 1971

G'n'L Sliced
Peaches
Byzantium, North Dakota
April 19, 1975

Generic Sliced Peaches
Nicety, Missouri
July 30, 1979

Oh-So-Good Sliced Peaches
Tantamount, New Mexico
June 11, 1982

Halcyon Sliced Peaches
East Pern, Idaho
December 1, 1985

R. Chast

ROZ CHAST

GET-WELL CARDS
for
UNDER-THE-WEATHER APPLIANCES

GET WELL SOON!

IN THE SHOP?

TO A SICK DRYER...

Contrast's gone?
Picture shot?
Don't know what it is
    you've got?
You'll soon be fixed,
    but even so
We miss your cheerful
    little glow.

Cold blows warm,
Hot blows cold.
Fact is, friend,
    you're getting old.
HOPE YOU'RE
REPAIRED SOON.

You burned a shirt,
You charred the socks,
You gave the folks electric
    shocks.

A leaky hose, a missing screw,
We hope that's all that's
    wrong with you.

R. Chast

MOM-O-GRAMS

♫ "You look too thin,
Your face is pale.
This is the path
That leads to jail."

♫ "Ask anyone who knows
    about science:
You don't use wet hands
    to unplug an
        appliance."

♫ "You live in a hovel,
It's really quite bleak.
You might try to vacuum
At least once a week." ♫

R. Chast

THEORIES OF EVERYTHING

STORES OF MYSTERY

Fred's Drugs

Surrounded by cut-rate drug-and-cosmetic emporiums that sell, let's say, a bottle of XYZ shampoo for 79¢. Same bottle at Fred's? $2.09 !!! How does he do it?

Beauty-Moi Frocks

Weird clothes, always five seasons out of date. Has been there forever. Store is usually pretty empty except for racks and racks of pants suits and the like. Who shops here?

M + O Typewriter Supplies

This place has been closed whenever one has walked by it. However, it's _always_ _there_, meaning somebody is continuing to pay rent on it. Why?

Tip-Top Goods

Boxes of saltines next to cartons of hair spray. Wigs, Christmas decorations, halter tops, institutional-sized jars of olives. Did all of this stuff "fall off a truck" or what?

R. Chast

ROZ CHAST

THE OBSERVATION DECK
OF APARTMENT 2-N

NEW YORK'S NEWEST NEIGHBORHOOD~
Little Vermont

VOODOO for TODAY

FOR GOOD HEALTH

Tie together a felt-tip pen, a chopstick, and a comb with seven missing teeth. Leave under couch.

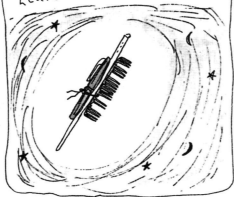

TO BECOME RICH

Crumple up a dollar bill and place it in the back left pocket of your favorite jeans. Wash and dry jeans until dollar has completely deteriorated.

TO MAKE SOMEONE FALL IN LOVE WITH YOU

In a food processor, combine 1 cup yogurt, ½ cup fabric softener, and a teaspoon of powdered after-dinner mints. Pour into Tupperware container and store in freezer until your wish comes true.

TO GET BACK AT SOMEONE

Without picking up the receiver, dial S-P-O-I-L-E-D-M-I-L-K on the telephone while thinking black thoughts about that person.

r. Chast

Welcome to... CAMP MANDATORY FUN!

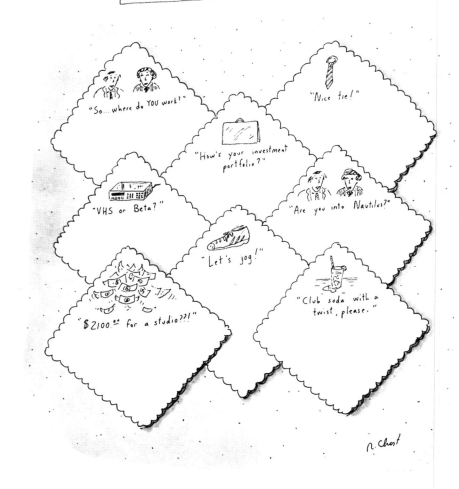

ROZ CHAST

June 1, 1987 THE NEW YORKER Price $1.75

THEORIES OF EVERYTHING

GRANTS & RECIPIENTS

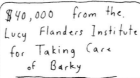

$25,000 from the Lucy and Ed Flanders Foundation for Going to Bed on Time

$40,000 from the Lucy Flanders Institute for Taking Care of Barky

$75,000 from the Ed Flanders Society for Growing Up Without Becoming Too Much of a Jerk

R. Chast

DISTRACTIONS OF THE GREAT

Here's Jane Austen. She's supposed to be writing, but she's getting her hair cut in _two hours!_

And Verdi. He's got an opera due in three weeks! But what about that chocolate cake in the pantry?

Henri Matisse was not at all immune, especially when it came to cats.

Why, this even happened to Madame Curie.

R. Chast

ROZ CHAST

Bob's Thoughts Fly Away

Mendelssohn's Concerto of the Exhausted in D-Minor, played by the Hackensack Symphony Orchestra...

La, la, la...

La, la... little duck falling off a ladder?

No, no... only the violinist... soup... WHO SAID SOUP? Cream of wheat...

What's that word spell? Oh... it's the curtain...

...Alexander, that's Nancy's son... the one with the Junior Mints...

...ha, ha, Ethel Merman's shoe... WAKE UP, BOB !!!

Lamb chops dressed in little skirts — Cellists... uh oh...

R. Chast

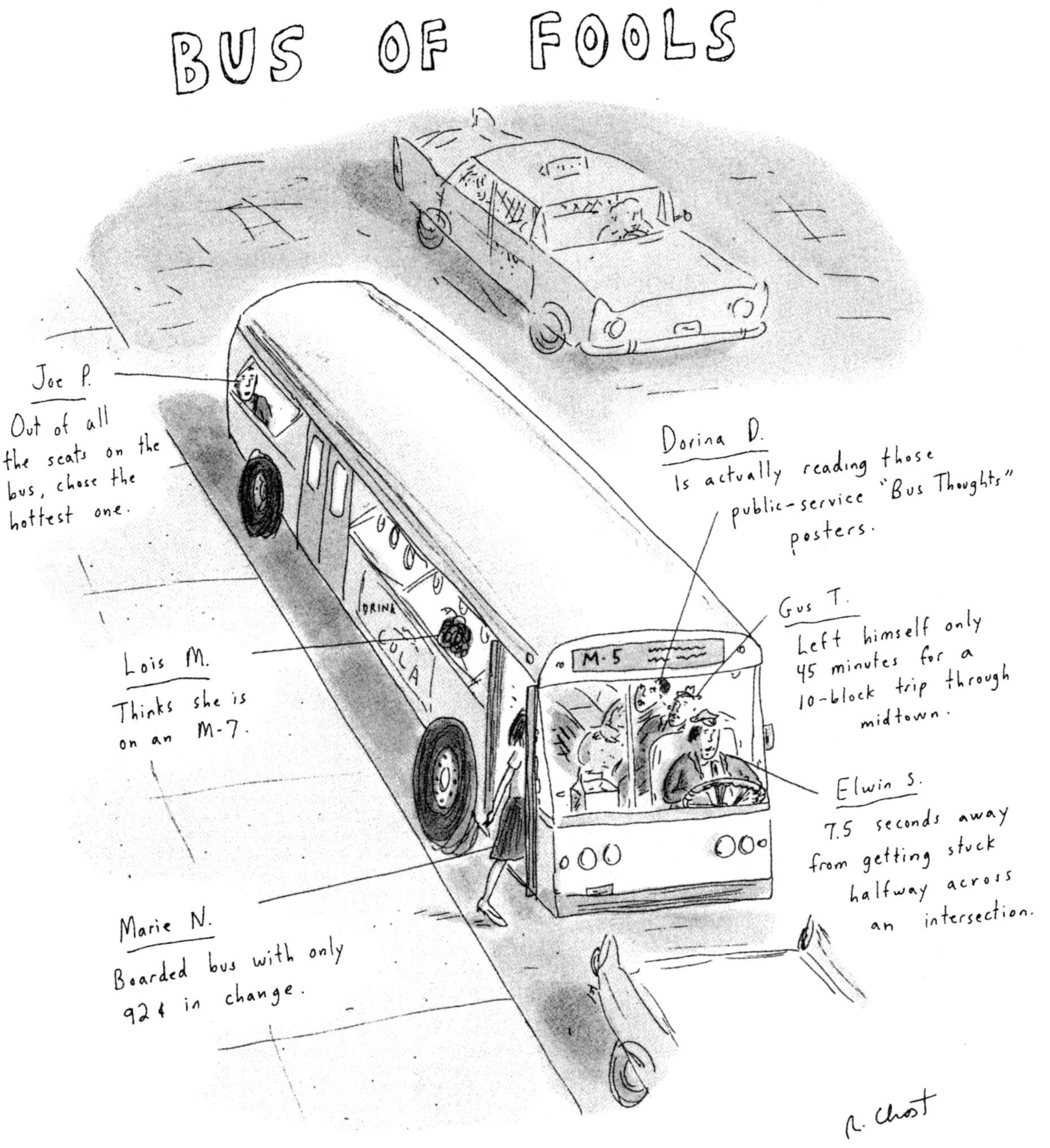

BUS OF FOOLS

Joe P.
Out of all the seats on the bus, chose the hottest one.

Dorina D.
Is actually reading those public-service "Bus Thoughts" posters.

Gus T.
Left himself only 45 minutes for a 10-block trip through midtown.

Lois M.
Thinks she is on an M-7.

Elwin S.
7.5 seconds away from getting stuck halfway across an intersection.

Marie N.
Boarded bus with only 92¢ in change.

R. Chast

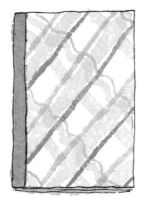

This book is
dedicated to

Doris   Boris
&
Morris   Cloris

copyright 1997
by the
KLIEGLIGHT
CORPORATION

ELLEN JAY
FLANDERS'
A
NEW
YORK
EVENING

The air was season-
ably cold and
everyone (almost) was
dressed appropriately.

It was not winter
in Moscow, but it
may as well
have been,

except that in
the chilly air,
Manhattan glittered
like a diamond

Everybody who was
anybody was on
their way to the
castle that night.

The Duchess
of Oats would
surely be there.

← Tiara
(worth
an arm
and a
leg!)

As well as
Count Clothesely.

Hopefully, the
Baron and Baroness
Von Hodgepodge
would arrive!

Others invited were the Duke of Strange

and the Marquis of the Van Allen Belt.

A little servant wearing some lovely togs came around bearing refreshments.

Then everyone took their seats in the main dining hall.

First course was a wonderful, clear broth of truffles—

served with a delightful bread.

An interesting pasta was then brought to the table by a host of tiny beings,

followed by a salad that was grown on the castle grounds.

Everyone partook of the delightful cookies.

Men and women alike retired to the library for brandy and a smoke.

The conversation drifted from Angola to circular farming,

to how much everyone despised goldfish

to Venice in the Fall, after the tourists left.

All too soon, everyone rang for their chauffeurs.

Fred

GOOD NIGHT, EVERYBODY!

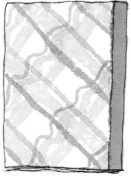

CHILDREN'S PERSONALS

NEW IN NBRHD –
Just moved in. Girl, 9, wishes to meet other girls, 8-10. Likes Barbie, Ken, Skipper. Box 101.

BOY W/ICKY PARENTS –
I need a rebellious peer group, ages 10-12. Serious replies only. Box 215.

GIRL, 4, LOOKING FOR IMGNRY FRIEND –
Humans need not apply. Photo a must. Box 643.

R. Chast

RADIATOR COOKERY

Flounder: 2 days

Potato: 3 weeks, 5 days

12 lb. roast: 4 months, 9 days

R. Chast

ROZ CHAST

DORIS K. ELSTON

BRAIN SURGEON · PROFESSIONAL
MODEL · ARTIST · LAWYER ·
plus
MOTHER OF FOUR

R. Chast

Approval Heaven

Compliments from
telephone operators

You *really* know
how to hold
up your end
of a conver-
sation, sir!

Positive feedback
from delivery guys

Very nice choice of
toppings,
Ma'am!

Pats on the back from
record-store clerks

Man, this is the coolest
selection of platters I've
seen in
months!

R. Chast

JUST FIGUREHEADS

Grand Kingfish of All the Prussias

Queen Doris of Indiana

Chief Bub of the Bronx

ROZ CHAST

THE JUKES AND THE KALLIKAKS

TODAY

Ed Jukes –
prominent real-estate developer

Amanda Kallikak –
attorney for Pastoral Nuclear
Waste Manufacturers, Inc.

Lance Kallikak –
hot young graffiti artist

Judy Ann Jukes –
newest queen of workout videos

R. Chast

THE NERVOUS GOURMET

This week: **LOW-RISK CHICKEN**

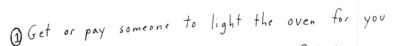

① Get or pay someone to light the oven for you

② Place chicken in oven using six-foot tongs.

③ Bake it for 1-1½ hours while you are close enough to make sure that the heat from the oven isn't setting anything on fire, but far enough away so that if, by any chance, the oven should explode, you will escape with only minor injuries.

④ Make arrangements to have someone remove chicken from oven while you stand at the opposite end of the kitchen.

⑤ Put on oven mitt and turn off oven.

YOUR FRIEND

Next week: **TOAST WITHOUT ANXIETY**

n. Chast

ROZ CHAST

PROFILES IN COURAGE

Asked total stranger next to him in movie theatre if he could possibly keep his voice to a whisper!

"mm mm?"

Did not side with crabby lady having argument with check-out girl in supermarket!

"Blah-blah-blah-blah... am I right???"
"No."

Entered exclusive boutique knowing she wasn't about to buy anything, and tried on an outfit costing $14,000!

"I just don't think it's me."

R. Chast

YOUNG PROFESSIONAL RECIPE TEST

Does recipe contain at least 4 different kinds of "flavored vinegars"?

¼ tsp. raspberry vinegar
¼ tsp. blueberry vinegar
⅛ tsp. champagne vinegar
¼ tsp. garlic vinegar

Does it require one tremendously expensive ingredient that you will use just this once and never again for as long as you live?

Essence of Macadamia Oil

Do you have to go out and buy a type of pan you've never even heard of?

"Do you carry Quäsenbö pans?"

R. Chast

THEORIES OF EVERYTHING

THINGS *NOT* TO TELL YOUR KID

Sometimes we drink milk from cows and sometimes we drink milk from horses like the ones in Central Park.

There's a big stopper at the bottom of the ocean, and every once in a while it gets accidentally pulled out.

Isn't this FUN?

"The Wizard of Oz" is a true story.

Anything electrical can suddenly BLOW UP for no reason whatsoever.

TICK
TICK
TICK
TICK

r. Chast

DIARY OF A CAT

TODAY
Today I got some food in a bowl. It was great! I slept some, too

TODAY
Played with yarn. Got some food in a bowl. Had a good nap

TODAY
Slept, food, yarn. Fun!

TODAY
I played with a shoelace. Ate, slept. A good day.

TODAY
Slept. Ate some food. Yum.

TODAY
Food in a bowl. Yarn galore. Dozed for quite a while.

TODAY
Had a good nap. Then food in a bowl. Then yarn.

r. Chast

UNWISE INVESTMENTS

Stumblebum

SIRED BY: CLUMSY OAF
OUT OF: LADY UH-OH

Galloping Consumption

SIRED BY: MISTER PROUST
OUT OF: PENICILLIN

Molasses in January

SIRED BY: BUMP ON A LOG
OUT OF: JUST DOZING

R. Chast

WHAT WENT WRONG?

Never owned dog?

Had strange middle name?

Johnny Xerxes Miller

Did not learn to play a musical instrument?

Too much fruit salad in early life?

R. Chast

ROZ CHAST

IT'S TIME FOR <u>YOU</u> TO START BANKING AT THE

FIRST NATIONAL ARTISTE SAVINGS & LOAN

Friendly tellers who will never, <u>ever</u> laugh at you.

Special loans having nothing to do with real estate or cars.

Interesting, unbourgeois premiums.

Signed Dali lithograph (unframed)

Recently reissued Ornette Coleman record

Paperback of Walt Whitman's poems

Officers who understand your particular set of problems.

IT'S THE HIGHWAY FOR PEOPLE WHO HATE TO DRIVE

"All those trucks careening toward you at 90 m.p.h.— it makes me sick!"

"What if you get lost?"

"What if the steering wheel comes off in your hands?"

"I hate it— I just hate the whole idea of it!"

INTRODUCING THE

POKY LITTLE PARKWAY

This is great!

- 5 lanes in either direction: SLOW, REALLY SLOW, INCREDIBLY SLOW, CRAWL, and STANDSTILL
- Maximum speed— 25 m.p.h.
- Each lane is 40 ft. wide and separated from the one next to it by a 3 ft. wide "mistake aisle"
- Drivers are alerted to each exit WELL IN ADVANCE
- No trucks
- No passing

So buckle up, calm down, and HEAD FOR THE OPEN ROAD!

a. chast

THE STORY OF
THE BOWL

Walking along the street, you might see in the window of a junk shop a type of bowl that in the back of your mind you remember is called "Yelloware."

Now, you don't collect this, or any other sort of bowl, and you are not even all that crazy about antiques, but you ask the price of it anyhow.

$15.00

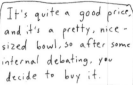

It's quite a good price, and it's a pretty, nice-sized bowl, so after some internal debating, you decide to buy it.

O.K., that sounds fine.

All the way home, you get more and more excited about the greatness of your purchase.

I'm so GLAD I spotted that bowl! It's such a neat bowl!!! I love that blue stripe around it!!! I was really in my right mind when I bought it!!!! I'd really be KICKING MYSELF if I hadn't

It was cheap, it's really cute, it's Yelloware, it's this, it's that, etc., etc., etc.

I can't believe it was only $15.00 for real Yelloware!!!! What a deal!!!! I'll put it up on that shelf near the spaghetti pot!!!!!!

When you're almost at your door, the bag it's in just taps an iron fence, but ever so lightly. Besides, the bowl is insulated in newspaper.

KLONK

You enter your place and finally unwrap your now almost supernaturally terrific new possession~

which is now lying there in 6 or 7 pieces. It is ALMOST TOO MUCH TO BEAR

From now on, every time you pass the Store of the Bowl, you will get a little nauseous.

JUNK

r. Chast

How Much Should You Tip?

SALESPEOPLE

10% of purchase price is adequate, but 15% is *gracious*

GRATUITIES

TEACHERS

20% of tuition at the end of the semester is the usual amount

POURBOIRES

LANDLORDS

25% of rent at Christmastime is deemed appropriate in most circles

ELM STREET — TENANTS · 59 EAST

R. Chast

Supplementary Scarlet Letters

Non-Jogger

NJ

Poor Credit Risk

PCR

Computer Illiterate

CI

R. Chast

THE WORLD'S SILLIEST IDEAS

The entire <u>universe</u> could be inside the sandwich of some huge being about to have us for lunch!

There is no reason to doubt that all Heaven and Earth is squished into a piece of dust on the needle of a phonograph belonging to a large organism!

Life as we know it could be going on in a gigantic alien child's pencil case that fell behind a bookcase!

Our existence could be taking place inside of an immense wastepaper basket!

<u>It</u> is possible that everything in our cosmos is happening in an unimaginably colossal person's discarded hatbox!

What if our being was occurring in the space between the pen point and the cap on a pen in the jacket pocket of a very <u>very</u>, <u>very</u> big humanoid?

R. Chast

MINI·REBELLIONS

If someone is forcing you to eat peas, take one and place it under a rug

When writing a thank-you note for a disliked gift, make a lot of spelling and grammatical mistakes.

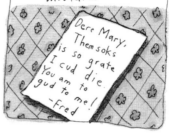

As you are dressing for a party you can't get out of attending, put on your least favorite tie or pin.

Pay a rude cabdriver with very old, torn, dirty money.

R. Chast

NEW TITLES FROM

BAD SEED HOUSE

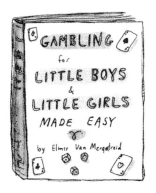

GAMBLING for LITTLE BOYS & LITTLE GIRLS MADE EASY
by Elmer Van Mergatroid

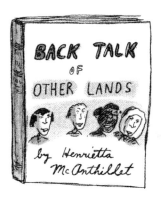

BACK TALK OF OTHER LANDS
by Henrietta McAnthillet

Myra Meringe Pye's HOW TO GET LOST IN A BIG STORE

Elsie Sapwither's 101 COMPLETELY TRUMPED-UP REASONS FOR NOT GOING TO SCHOOL
It's too hot!

DISGUSTING SONGS TO SING WHILE PEOPLE ARE EATING
compiled by Alice and Eric Fidget

A Living Hell: WHAT I TURNED MY PARENTS' LIVES INTO
by Salmonella Sumpins

R·Chast

SOCIAL CONTRACTS

Bob will not step on Joe's toe simply because it has crossed his mind to do so.

Mary will not set Betty Lou's hair afire even if it really gets on her nerves.

Tom will not plow his car through the Bakers' house although they deserve it.

R. Chast

THE SENSITIVE CHILD

Sticks and stones
May break my bones,
But words will stay with me
forever as they sit inside
me, getting turned over and over,
being blown completely out of proportion.

R. Chast

HIGHLIGHTS FROM THE ANNUAL
CENTRAL PARK COUNTRY FAIR

Come see brawny Akitas pull
many times their weight
in Sunday papers!

Admire prize-winning produce
culled by entrants from Korean
markets throughout the 5-borough area!

Up on Machinery Hill, you'll be
able to inspect state-of-the-art
food processors, pasta makers,
and VCR equipment!

And visit the numerous "All-You-
Can-Eat-of-French-Haute-Cuisine"
stands—they're _always_ a big hit!

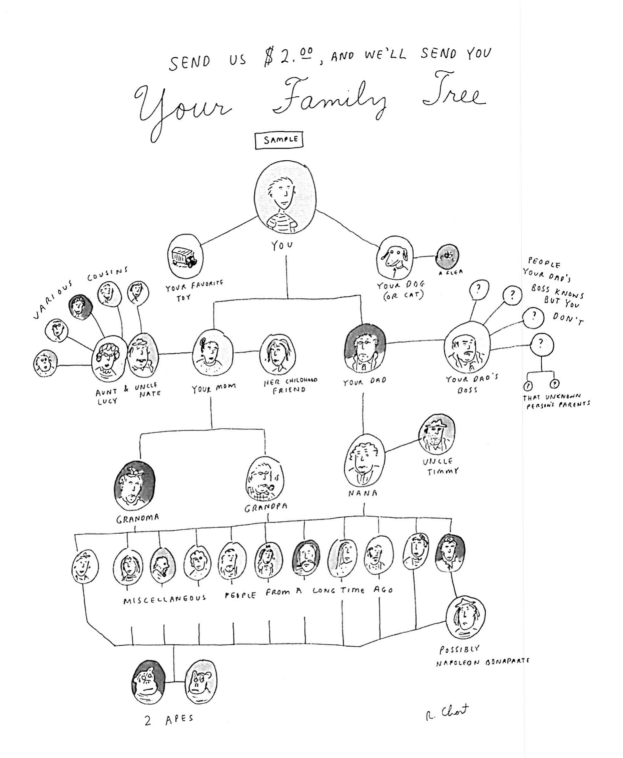

SEND US $2.00, AND WE'LL SEND YOU

Your Family Tree

ROZ CHAST

RECIPES FROM THE "I REALLY, REALLY HATE TO COOK" COOKBOOK

Lunchtime Surprise

6 old green olives
5/6 plum
3½ slices yellow American cheese
8 oyster crackers
bite of cheesecake
⅓ c. rice pudding
10 Necco wafers
Serves 1.

12 - Second Casserole

Throw a bunch of unspoiled stuff in a pot that won't blow up when you put it in the oven. Bake till hot. Serves 1.

Leftover Jamboree

Leftovers
Water

Do your best to find a clean pan. Heat food up with a little water. Serves 1.

Ma Bell's Special

Takeout menu
Telephone

Decide what you're in the mood for. Dial. Order. Wait for delivery. Serves 1.

Chinese?

Pizza?

R. Chast

USEFUL DEGREES

Bachelor of Waitressing (B.W.)

Bachelor of Grocery Arts (B.G.A.)

Bachelor of Clothing-Display Science (B.C.D.S.)

Bachelor of Lotto (B.L.)

THANK YOU FOR JOINING THE LIMITED-ATTENTION-
SPAN BOOK CLUB HERE IS YOUR FIRST NOVEL:

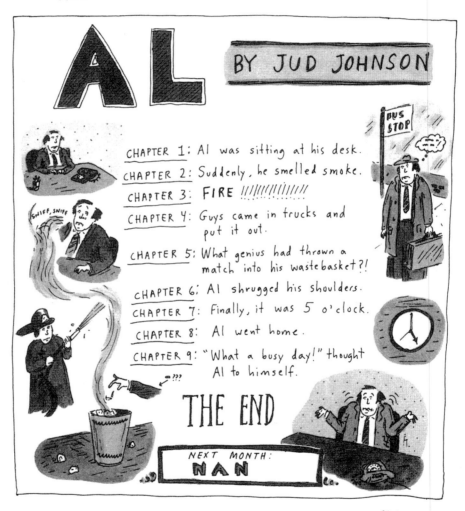

AL BY JUD JOHNSON

CHAPTER 1: Al was sitting at his desk.

CHAPTER 2: Suddenly, he smelled smoke.

CHAPTER 3: **FIRE** ////////////////

CHAPTER 4: Guys came in trucks and put it out.

CHAPTER 5: What genius had thrown a match into his wastebasket?!

CHAPTER 6: Al shrugged his shoulders.

CHAPTER 7: Finally, it was 5 o'clock.

CHAPTER 8: Al went home.

CHAPTER 9: "What a busy day!" thought Al to himself.

THE END

NEXT MONTH: **NAN**

SECRETS
OF ADULTHOOD

Anybody can change a light bulb

Soap and water will take most stains right out

One shampoo is just about as good as another.

The word "cosine" never, ever comes up

99.9% of people don't understand tides.

It's o.k. to throw out a pencil whenever you feel like it

R. Chast

Lifetime Achievement Awards

Named for living well within her means since 1931.

Recognized for never missing a 6-month dental checkup since 1948.

Honored for looking at the bright side since 1955

r. Chst

Miss Ilene Kranshaw sings
100% GRAMMATICALLY CORRECT POPULAR TUNES

FEATURING:

"(You Aren't Anything but a) Hound Dog"

"It Doesn't Mean a Thing If It Hasn't Got That Swing"

—and—

"I'm Not Misbehaving"

r. Chst

ROZ CHAST

FORGET YOUR WORRIES AT...

VELTON CORNERS SPA

We feature...

MILK BATHS (IF THAT'S WHAT YOU REALLY WANT)

EXERCISE CLASSES WITH PAULINE AND PAT

HEALTHFUL, NO-NONSENSE MEALS COOKED BY PAULINE HERSELF

THE FAMOUS WATERS OF VELTON CORNERS

R. Chast

THE TRUE STORY OF
VANILLA PUDDING

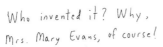

Who invented it? Why, Mrs. Mary Evans, of course!

Did you buy anything?

Let me see..... No, I did not.

And what *were* the Circumstances, exactly?

I think it was a Tuesday...

By the way, where does Mrs. Golgarsh come into this?

That woman is the biggest recipe thief for miles around. She does not come into this *at* *all.*

And *then* what happened?

The doorbell rang. Somebody was selling something.

Why do you call it "vanilla pudding"?

Well, when I tasted it, it tasted just like vanilla pudding. Hence its name.

r. Chast

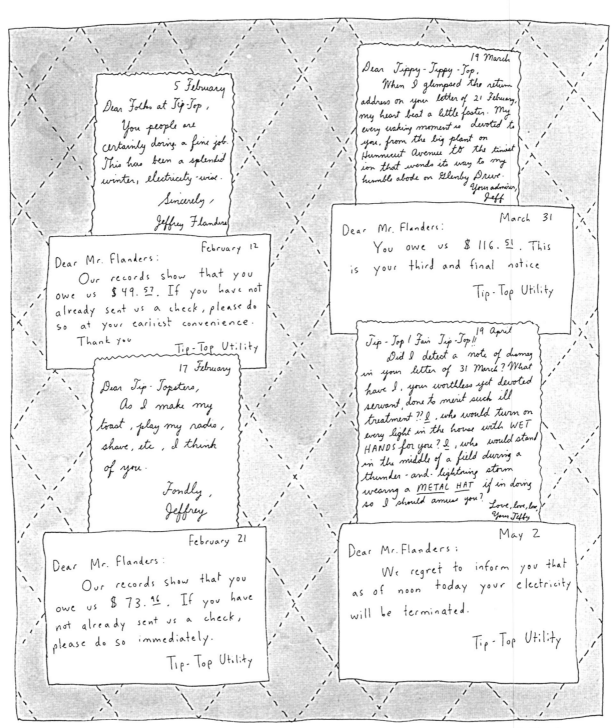

ROZ CHAST

KWALITY TIME

When The Cat's Away, The Mice Will...

The SPONTANEOUS GOURMET

"Sometimes something happens ... and sometimes it doesn't."

1. In a small pan, sauté ½ c. onion in 2 tbsp. oil or butter.
2. Heat a can of tomato soup to just below a boil.
3. Sift ¾ c. flour.
4. Pound flat 6 chicken breasts.
5. Add ⅓ c. raisins to 1 egg and let sit overnight.
6. Measure ⅛ tsp. nutmeg.
7. Crumble 14 soda crackers.
8. Grate 2 c. cheddar cheese.
9. Remove the casing from 1 lb. sweet Italian sausage.
10. Take 30 maraschino cherries.

R Chast

If you're interested in entering the high-paying world of
TV journalism, first you must learn

THE ART OF BANTERING!

You'll learn about:

- The ever-popular weather banter
- News bantering: which topics are good, which topics are maybe not so good
- Holiday bantering
- What to do when you hit a "banter wall": EMERGENCY BANTER
- Free-form bantering (for the advanced)

SIMPLY CHECK ONE:

☐ Yes, please send me my Banter Info-Pak
☐ No, I'd rather not know one tiny thing more about this topic

R. Chast

FROM THE TOURNAMENT OF NEUROSES PARADE

The "I Never Really Broke Away from My Parents" Float

The "In My Mind's Eye, I Will Always Be a Fat, Short, Frizzy-Haired, Glasses-and-Braces-Wearing Sixth Grader" Float

The "People Who Have Difficulty Forming Bonds of Intimacy with Other People" Float

The "I Only Want What Is Unattainable" Float

The "Hypochondria" Float

The "Fear of Chickens" Float

ROZ CHAST

r. Chost

FOR THE NEW GARDENER

 # 3017 Plant Comb and Brush Set —
Keep your greenery looking spry. Order now and we'll throw in some shampoo.

$22.00

 # 6338 Anti-Dandelion Cassette —
Voice intones, "Dandelions, BEGONE!" for 90 minutes. The results will astonish you.

$10.00

 # 4629 Specialty Shovels —
You don't really need these, and you don't even know what they're for, do you? Go ahead, get them anyway.

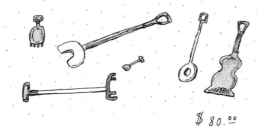

$ 80.00

#8028 Low-Fat Plant Food —
If you care at all about your plants, this is what you'll feed them.

Methuselah LOW-FAT PLANT FOOD
MIX WITH WATER

$7.50

 # 5780 Expert Gardener's Outfit —
Once you get the "look" right, everything else will surely fall into place.

professional gardener's hat

old clothes

special clogs

$195.00

 # 9976 Glue-on Flowers —
For when all else fails.

BEFORE   AFTER

$ 18.00

r.Cht

THE CRADLE OF MANKIND

FAILED LAUNDRY DETERGENTS

The detergent that tries to persuade dirt that it really isn't wanted and should therefore leave.

The soap flakes that _totally ignore_ dirt in the hope that it will go away.

The cleanser that tells dirt that unless it dissolves this instant there will be hell to pay.

ROZ CHAST

LORE AND LEGEND OF THE PENNYPACKERS

How Great-Grandpa Louie Came to America with $12.00 in His Pocket and Eventually Owned a Baking Soda Factory

The Time the Ferris Wheel Got Stuck for an Hour and Aunt Pearl and Uncle Barney Were in the Top Car

The Story of Grandma Iris's Terrible Ear Infection Back in the Days Before There Was Such a Thing as Penicillin

Cousin Gladys's Psychic Dream That Showed the Exact Location of Her Friend Doris Benson's Lost Pair of Pinking Shears

Aunt Tessie's Date with Errol Flynn's Second Cousin

How the Connors Branch of the Family Found Itself in Hoboken, New Jersey

PROOF OF
LIFE ON EARTH

Last week's issue of a TV magazine

A chicken casserole

An eight-page letter from Aunt Bonnie describing Uncle Carl's operation

Cousin Jimmy's intramural-basketball-playoff trophy

Pocket lint

Photo of a friend of Aunt Bonnie with Dexter, age 19½

Unopened jar of mayonnaise

Notebooks galore

A sofa pillow

This hereby certifies that _____ is actually here on this very planet. Signed, _____ NOTARY PUBLIC
DATE _____ YOUR NAME _____

Sworn statement by a notary public

R. Chast

HIGHLIGHTS for ADULTS:
OUR OWN PAGE

Self-Portrait

Debbi Sue Dunkirk, age 39
North Pin, N.J.

My Favorite Horse

Jim Delancy, age 56³/₄
Happy Springs, Fla.

Unlucky Ticket

Carla McCoy, age 60½
Temtee, N.Y.

My Husband

Jeanine Briscomb, age 42
Tossup, N.C.

One Day Last Week

Don Whitmore, age 49½
East Parkette, Del.

Dwayne's X-Ray

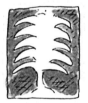

Lucille Knapp, age 63¼
Dewey, Ark.

Our New Satellite Dish
With Bob

Denise Prescott, age 36½
New Meal, Kan.

Me, After I Lost 325 Lbs.

Polly Walker, age 40³/₄
Hewlitt, Ohio

My Boss

Ed Camberly, age 57
Wheelerten Basin, N.D.

R. Chast

IN THE FINAL ANALYSIS

As much as people go on and on about horses, they are still very large and have weird teeth.

There's a limit to what even the most expensive, top-of-the-line cosmetics can do.

Cauliflower will never taste as good as chocolate.

Everybody's apartment has a tragic flaw.

There's no light.

There are no closets.

It's in Passaic.

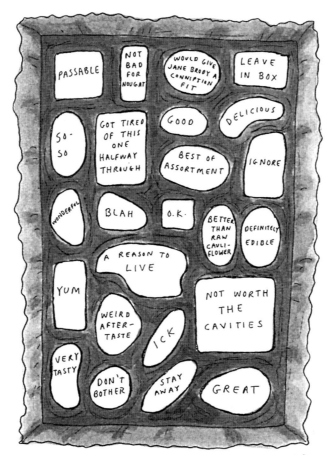

HADLEY K., ALL-DAY SUCKER

R. Chast

8:00 A.M. ~ Woke up. Ate oat bran followed by tons of vitamins.

8:37 A.M. ~ Called and pledged $100.⁰⁰ to the Your Condo in Heaven Foundation.

9:12 A.M. ~ Went outside, played a little three-card monte

11:00 A.M. ~ Attended "Vortex Mind Control" Seminar at New York Penta.

12:39 P.M. ~ Bought Cartier watch from street vender.

1:00 P.M. ~ Lunch: paid $19.⁰⁰ for spaghetti and meatballs.

2:02 P.M. ~ Bought Vuitton luggage from street vender.

2:26 P.M. ~ Went home; talked to Aunt Shelley; got into argument over whether or not she was thanked for socks she gave me four years ago, let her win.

3:00 P.M. ~ Aromatherapy class.

5:21 P.M. ~ Gave money to guy collecting for the Save the Chrysler Building Foundation.

7:00 P.M. ~ Dinner: paid $35.⁰⁰ for hamburger and French fries.

8:18 P.M. ~ Went home. Agreed to write 50,000-word article on cold fusion for $25.⁰⁰.

9:09 P.M. ~ Ordered shoes from a catalogue.

10:36 P.M. ~ Read book on channelling.

12:11 A.M. ~ Slept on special orthopedic pillow while listening to "Learn French Overnight" cassette.

ROZ CHAST

THE ART OF THE DEAL
by Uncle Sidney
CHAPTER 7: THE BUSINESS LUNCH

Step One:
Admire something the other guy is wearing.

Say, that's SOME TIE!

Step Two:
Share a funny story about yourself.

Let me tell you how I got my driver's license.

Step Three:
Look for something in common.

So, do you ever watch Carson?

Step Four:
Make observations about somebody else's business acumen with materials at hand.

Whoever invented these must be making a pretty penny.

Step Five:
Suddenly, get deep.

Doesn't all this sometimes seem absurd to you?

Step Six:
Go in for the kill.

But enough of this idle chitchat.

R. Chst

FUSSBUDGET 1989

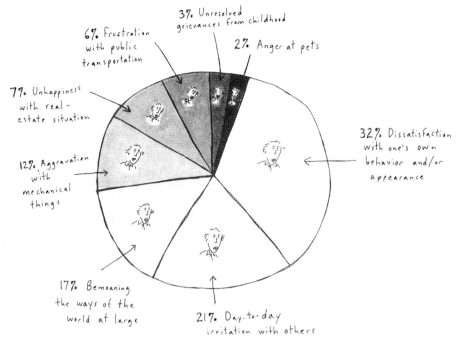

3% Unresolved grievances from childhood

6% Frustration with public transportation

2% Anger at pets

7% Unhappiness with real-estate situation

12% Aggravation with mechanical things

32% Dissatisfaction with one's own behavior and/or appearance

17% Bemoaning the ways of the world at large

21% Day-to-day irritation with others

r. Cht

Why One's Parents Got Married

A really convincing guy told them that if they tied the knot they'd get a zillion dollars _and_ learn all the secrets of the cosmos...

Sounds good to me!

Me, too!

An alien civilization threatened to blow up the planet unless the two were wed.

They _were_, in fact, for a brief time, the only man and woman on Earth, except for a nearby justice of the peace.

I do.

I do.

r. Chast

WHY OIL SPILLS ARE GOOD
BY D. ALVIN ARMBRUSTER, C.E.O., ABC OIL CORPORATION

① EVERY ONCE IN A WHILE, IT'S GOOD TO GIVE THE OCEANS' SELF-CLEANING MECHANISMS A REAL WORKOUT. IT'S LIKE TAKING YOUR CAR FOR A LONG, FAST DRIVE ON A SUMMER AFTERNOON.

② OIL-COATED BIRDS ARE BETTER PROTECTED AGAINST THE SUN'S RAYS THAN NON-OIL-COATED BIRDS.

③ LAB TESTS PROVE THAT MANY UNDERWATER PLANTS ACTUALLY _LOVE_ THE TASTE OF PETROLEUM!

④ A RUINED FISHING INDUSTRY MEANS THAT PEOPLE WILL GO BACK TO EATING MORE MEAT, AMERICA'S MOST VIRILE FOOD

⑤ PEOPLE IN THE MEDIA ALSO BENEFIT! SPILL-VIDEOTAPERS, INTERVIEWERS OF BIRD-WASHERS, ECOLOGICAL-DISASTER PREDICTORS, ETC. — WITHOUT US, WHERE WOULD _THEY_ BE?

ROZ CHAST

The Very Last Dinosaur

IN DEEP DENIAL

ANCIENT LANDMARKS

OF NEW YORK CITY

Scaffold, West 81st Street
Is believed to have originated in the early 12th century A.D.

Sidewalk Crater, Amsterdam Avenue
Has been there since the time of the Pharaohs.

Half-Deconstructed Town House, East 19th Street
References to it have been found in the Old Testament.

Abandoned Automobile, Riverside Drive
Fragments have been carbon-dated to the Jurassic period.

R. Chast

ROZ CHAST

ODD SPAS

ON DISPLAY AT THE

CHILDREN'S HOUSE OF HORRORS

The Hall of Snowsuits

The Plate Where All the Different Foods Are Touching One Another

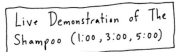

The Gallery of Inexplicable Fears

Live Demonstration of The Shampoo (1:00, 3:00, 5:00)

R. Chast

BARTLETT'S UNFAMILIAR QUOTATIONS

"Never wear white after Labor Day."
— Plato

"Once the transmission goes, the whole car goes."
— William Shakespeare

"It's better to own than to rent."
— Sigmund Freud

ED GOES GREEN

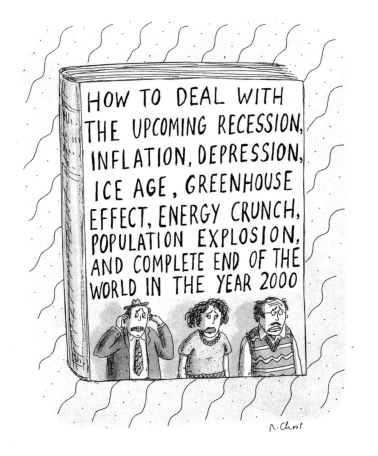

THEORIES OF EVERYTHING

CASH MACHINES from ACROSS THE LAND

The Big Purse
East Lubbock, New Jersey

Dad's Pocket Casheteria
Twelve Buckets, Nebraska

The Weeping Bankbook
Hensteeth, Alabama

Mattress o' Moola
Knorl, Idaho

R. Chast

Bartlett's Expanded Quotations

"Sally is the pretty one, June is the smart one."
~ May Lipton

"I could have bought an entire brownstone for $12,000 in those days."
—Ralph Sims

"So you think the world owes you a living, is that right?"
—Mr. and Mrs. Edgewater

SIGNS OF THE TIMES

A boxful of arugula goes bad at the Westview Market in Manhattan.

A de-luxe coffee-, espresso-, and cappuccino-maker is dredged up from the Hudson River.

In a secret rite at Battery Park City, eight men burn their yellow ties.

Somewhere, an aerobics class folds.

SALLY SUE'S 6 A.M. EARLY-BIRD ADVANCED SUPER-HIGH-ENERGY AEROBICS CLASS HAS BEEN CANCELLED.

MILLIE'S GEAR SLIPS

One day, the family set off on a little car trip.

"Everybody ready?"

They were just about to leave when Millie realized she'd forgotten her sweater.

"Oops! I'll be right back!"

It took her about four minutes and eleven seconds to get the sweater and return to the car.

"Okeydokey! Now we're all set."

As they were driving, she thought, This is exactly the place I would have been four minutes and eleven seconds ago, but now it's slightly different, and I'll never see what I was _supposed_ to see.

She realized she would always be _exactly_ _that_ _little space of time behind._

MY LIFE NOW = (MY REAL LIFE) − (FOUR MINUTES + ELEVEN SECONDS)!

In the supermarket, she thought, Normally I would have been in Aisle Three, but here I am, amongst the produce.

In a line at the movies, she knew herself always to be about two or three places behind her _real_ place.

It was sort of horrendous, as there was really no way to fix this kind of thing.

However, as the years passed she grew accustomed to it.

ROZ CHAST

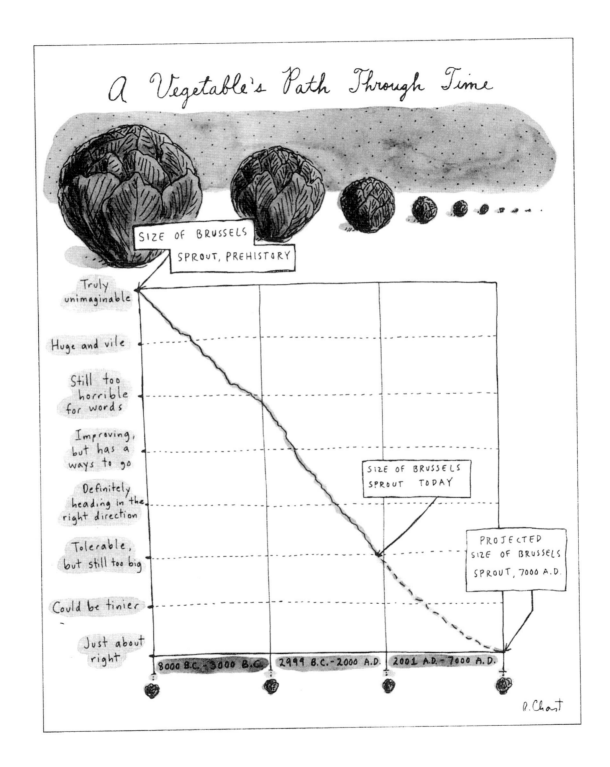

THE ADVENTURES OF
WIMP MOM

There are definitely times of the day when one's three-year-old may be in a horrible mood.

Who knows what the Tough Mom might do to stop that sort of thing?

NOW YOU STAY IN YOUR ROOM UNTIL YOU'RE READY TO ACT LIKE A **HUMAN BEING, PAL!**

If you are a Wimp Mom, perhaps you will try to distract your kid in a calm, soothing manner.

Honeybunch, let's go over to the couch and *READ ABOUT DINO-SAURS!*

ALL YOU WANT TO KNOW ABOUT DINOSAURS

You are lucky if this works for ten seconds.

"Dinosaurs were very, very big."

Often, you will only find yourself in deeper and hotter water.

NO, THEY WEREN'T!!!

What a wimpy, wimpy Mom.

O.K., they weren't big. They were as tiny as peas.

R. Chst

TIME·TO·SPARE.
BOOK CLUB

ALL·DAY RECIPES
by Doris Pettigrew

HOW TO MAKE YOUR CHILDREN SHOES FROM SCRATCH
by Sam and Susan Jenkins
OVER 250 PATTERNS INSIDE!

HOOKING HUGE AREA RUGS
for every room in the house
by Gloria Kirby

IRONING & MAINTAINING DOLL CLOTHING
by Eunice Glasworthy

THE FORGOTTEN ART of FRUIT ARRANGEMENT
by Catherine Sloan

THROW A CARNIVAL IN YOUR BACKYARD
by Missy Krenshaw

R·Chst

ROZ CHAST

What Children Overhear

...She bent down to pick up the pencil, and when she stood up, she was BLIND IN HER LEFT EYE.

...When he woke up, his feet had swollen to the size of WATERMELONS.

...Her scalp became infected, so they had to remove it.

...His fingernails all fell off, one by one.

...They drilled a hole in his larynx and put in a pipe that stretched CLEAR ACROSS THE ROOM.

...Mrs. Cleary's son was born with two stomachs, but he didn't find out til he was thirty-six.

R. Chast

TIME-OFF COUPONS

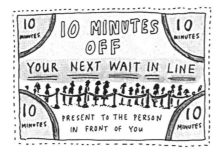

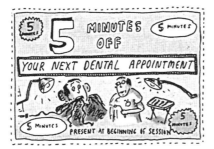

WHERE THE ECOLOGICALLY CORRECT
MEETS THE PATHOLOGICALLY FRUGAL

SINCE YOU ASKED

Ingredients: snips, snails, snail by-products, puppy-dog tails, other puppy-dog by-products.

Ingredients: sugar, aspartame, spice, everything nice, a blend of nutritive and non-nutritive sweeteners.

DOWSING FOR COFFEE

ROZ CHAST

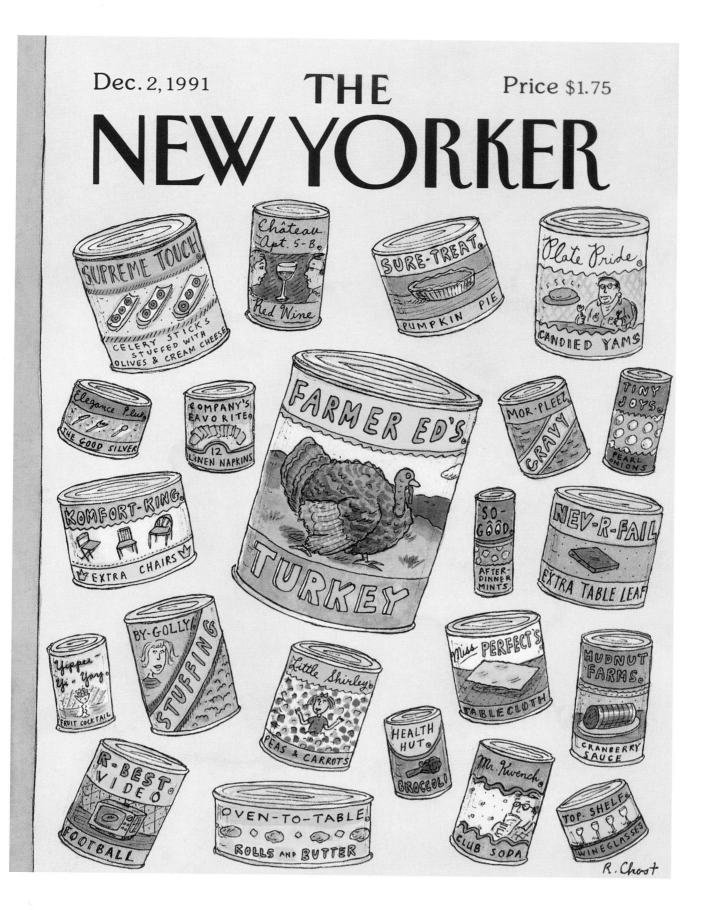

Frederick's OF WINNIPEG

#143 Flannel Two-Piece P.J.s ~

Warm, comfortable, machine wash/dry.
What more can you ask for?

#507 Electric Granny Gown ~

Say goodbye to winter's chill
with this extra-toasty sleepwear.

#639 His 'n' Hers Nightshirts ~

They'll pay for themselves within <u>one</u>
<u>month</u> on what you'll save on your
<u>heating bill</u> — OR YOUR MONEY BACK.

#805 Down Union Suit ~

Fasten yourself in one of these
some cold December eve, and you
won't want to emerge till May.

R. Chst

AFTER THE BREAKUP OF
BACCHUS, INC.

Ed, God of Red Wine

Judy, Goddess of White Wine

Charles, God of Rosé

Bobbi Jo, Goddess of Sherry, Port, and Passover-Type Wines

Ray, God of Wine Coolers

OUR PLANET

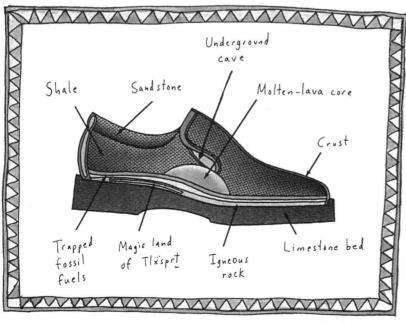

Underground cave

Shale   Sandstone   Molten-lava core

Crust

Trapped fossil fuels   Magic land of Tlïxsprt   Igneous rock   Limestone bed

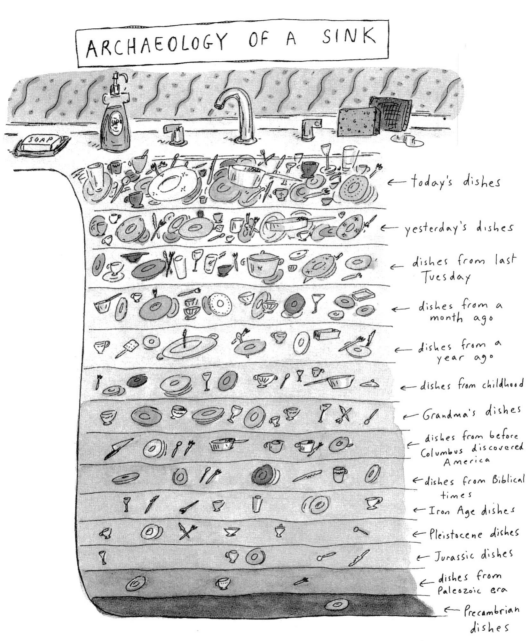

ARCHAEOLOGY OF A SINK

SOAP

← today's dishes

← yesterday's dishes

← dishes from last Tuesday

← dishes from a month ago

← dishes from a year ago

← dishes from childhood

← Grandma's dishes

← dishes from before Columbus discovered America

← dishes from Biblical times

← Iron Age dishes

← Pleistocene dishes

← Jurassic dishes

← dishes from Paleozoic era

← Precambrian dishes

R. Chst

ROZ CHAST

THE LITANY OF FUN

...and then we got on the bus and then we all had treats and then we sang songs and then we played games and then Billy and Kenny got into a fight over a Ninja and then we got off the bus and then we had a snack and then we stood in line and then we got tickets and then we went into the zoo and then we saw the Wild Africa exhibit and then we got back in line and then we saw the Hall of Bats exhibit and then we were talking and laughing and then we got back in line and then Mrs. Hudson got mad at us and then we got quieter and then we marched to the picnic tables and then we sat down and then some of us got hot dogs at the concession stand and then some of us got burgers with cheese and some of us got burgers without cheese and then we ate lunch and then we got back in line and then we went to the Wild World of Monkeys and then we went to Our Undersea Friends and then Mrs. Hudson yelled at us some more and then we had a snack under a tree and then we got back in line and then we went to the souvenir shop and then we bought monkey stickers or erasers that had bat heads or T-shirts that said "I've Been to Herkimer Zoo" or key chains with little whales hanging from them and then we walked back to Parking Lot B and then we got on the bus and then Mr. Jones drove us home and here I am.

r. Cheat

THE ANCIENT ENQUIRER

MAY 17, 8423 B.C.   FIFTY CENTS

WOMAN TURNS INTO PILLAR OF SALT!

HUSBAND LOOKS ON IN HORROR

see page 2

MAN LIVES FOR THREE DAYS IN WHALE'S STOMACH— AND SURVIVES!

see page 3 JONAH

TOP GREEK GOD GIVES BIRTH TO FULL-GROWN GAL— VIA HIS FOREHEAD!!!

see page 9 FATHER AND DAUGHTER, RESTING COMFORTABLY

EXCLUSIVE TO THE ANCIENT ENQUIRER: UNRETOUCHED PHOTOS OF THE WORLD'S ONLY **THREE-HEADED DOG!**

CERBERUS see centerfold for more pix

R. Clw

OPP'Y OF A LIFETIME

Fast-growing midtown corp needs bright, articulate M/F to reorganize 760,000 files from top to bottom, fire four people nobody else will, and take care of children aged three and one. Must be certified in UNEX, GOM, SYSCO, CREM, LEM, ZOT, FENIX, JOD, and FRON. Own car a necessity, also up-to-date trucking license. Knowledge of quantum physics, short-order cookery helpful. Can you type? Even better. If you have $250,000 cash and are not afraid of large dogs, we're looking for _You_. At least twelve years' experience required. Personable, attractive college grads only call 555-2121 for appt. Starting salary 9K. Great benefits.

R. Chast

RECYCLING IN HELL

by Roz Chast

SAFETY TIPS

FROM THE
AMERICAN COUNCIL TO AVOID STATIC SHOCKS

① Before touching metal doorknob with hand, touch knee to something metal, like the refrigerator.

② Get up really carefully from the couch to avoid accumulating extra electric particles.

③ Never, if you can help it, either purchase or walk upon a new wool carpet.

④ If you have indeed become static-laden, just sit on a nice wooden chair until it passes.

ROZ CHAST

ADDITIONS TO THE RAINBOW CURRICULUM

DON'T HOLD YOUR BREATH FOR ROBERT DE NIRO'S NEWEST TV SHOW

"KENWOOD PARK"

Kenwood Park, a Brooklyn neighborhood of two- and three-story buildings with apartments above car-repair places, run-down luncheonettes, laundromats, bars, and strange, sad dress shops...

...a neighborhood left behind by everything and everyone.

THIS WEEK:

Joe and Minnie go out grocery shopping.

We need cottage cheese.

We do **NOT** need cottage cheese.

Nora gets her hair done.

I want it to really, like, FLIP AROUND here.

Then perm the whole damn thing.

Lars, the super's boy, takes up his post in the lobby.

r. Chst

WELCOME TO — Are You All Right? — THEATRE

The curtain rises as we find Howard and Janine sitting on the couch.

Howard shifts his position and reaches for a tissue to blow his nose.

Suddenly, Janine inquires:

ARE YOU ALL RIGHT?

Twelve minutes pass. Janine clears her throat and closes her eyes for a second.

AHEM

Howard feels a wave of panic rise in him as he asks:

ARE YOU ALL RIGHT?

Things settle down. Howard stands up, uses the bathroom, and sits back down on the couch.

With tremendous anxiety and concern, Janine queries:

ARE YOU ALL RIGHT?

Finally, Janine sighs and says "I think I'll go upstairs and lie down for a little while" just as Howard examines a cuticle.

It's a moment charged with emotion as they ask each other:

ARE YOU ALL RIGHT?

— THE CURTAIN FALLS —

The End

R. Chast

ROZ CHAST

CITY CAMPS

Camp Ci-Ne-Mah
862 Irving Place

Boys and girls aged five to fifteen spend six weeks going from movie house to movie house. Activities include blockbusters, crime dramas, comedies, serious European films, and revivals.

Camp Shah-Ping
9631 Lexington Avenue

An unforgettable experience for children aged seven to fourteen. They'll make friends for life as they browse through New York's finest department stores and boutiques. Established 1924.

Camp Res-Toh-Rant
6475 East 89th Street

A wonderful summer lies ahead for campers aged six to fifteen. They will receive expert instruction in dealing with various cuisines, and also in making reservations, tipping, and paying by credit card.

I'd like to put this on Visa, please.

Camp In-Dor-O
1839 West End Avenue

Our forty-fifth year in this ten-room prewar apartment. A noncompetitive atmosphere for the quieter, less active child. We offer reading, coloring, TV, chess, Monopoly, lanyard-making, and more.

ROZ CHAST

RASHOMON OF WEST 84th STREET

The Guy Who Says He Saw the Parking Spot First

It's *MINE*, you life-ruiner.

I hope you rot in Hell forever, you lying son of a bitch.

The Gal Who Says She Saw the Parking Spot First

The Doorman from Across the Street

She's a troublemaker, just trying to take advantage of *poor Mr. Edwards*, one of the kindest, most generous tenants on this earth.

The Feminist Historian Who Saw the Whole Thing Happen from Her Window

This is sadly typical of the way men have behaved for centuries. It's *HERS.*

The Amateur Videotaper

If this gets really good, I'll sell it to "HARD COPY."

r. Chast

THE WORLD'S FIRST GENETICALLY ENGINEERED HUMAN HITS ADOLESCENCE

We buy you the best genes in the world— FOR THIS?

So, I got my nose pierced. So *what*, man.

I remember checking "genius" on the order form— *AND NOW LOOK!*

r. Chast

ROZ CHAST

HOW NOT TO REMEMBER NAMES

T.S. ELIOT MEETS BEAVIS AND BUTT-HEAD

ROZ CHAST

INTRODUCING...

Healing Truths

MOTHER'S DAY CARDS

To Mother

ON THIS VERY
SPECIAL DAY

→ You knew I wanted Barbie,
The world's most perfect teen.
Instead, you chose to buy me
A generic figurine.

Thanks for saving three dollars.

TO A DEAR PERSON

On Mother's Day

→ You did the best with the skills you had.
Considering everything, you weren't so bad.

I'll try not to repeat your mistakes.

WITH GOOD
WISHES ON
THIS DAY

TO MOM

→ Your house is always clean and neat,
Your lemon poundcake can't be beat.
Self-negating mom and wife,
It's not too late to get a life.

Only trying to help.

R. Chast

THE 60-HOUR GOURMET

RECIPES FOR PEOPLE WHO HAVE TIME TO SPARE, AND THEN SOME

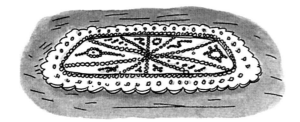

Painstakin' Peas

Before cooking, peel six hundred peas. Boil. Then arrange in a festive manner on a serving platter.

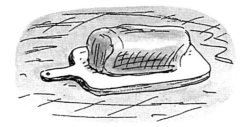

Never-Ending Bread

Mix bread dough as usual. Let rise until double. Punch down. Let rise again. Punch down. Let rise. Punch down. Let rise. Punch down. Rise. Punch. Rise, punch, rise, punch, rise. Bake and serve.

Slow 'n' Steady Chicken

Wash chicken in a lukewarm bubble bath for ± one hour. Then rinse for thirty minutes. Stuff with Difficult Stuffing*, using a doll spoon, and truss with an itsy-bitsy needle and the teensy-weensiest stitch you can. Cook at 125°F. for 32 hours. Just prior to serving, carve into the shape of a rose.
* see page 883

Handmade Carrot Juice

Begin by mincing raw carrots with a butter knife. Then keep going until the whole thing reaches a liquid consistency.

R. Chast

ROZ CHAST

APEX TOBACCO: AN INTERNAL MEMO

TO: ALL EMPLOYEES

RE: THE ELDERLY AS TARGET AUDIENCE

① Smoking can be enjoyed indoors, where the elderly spend a lot of time.

② It is a solitary activity, as opposed to square dancing or Scrabble.

③ Many old people smoked in their youth, so:

    A) it won't be a thing they'll have to learn from scratch, and

    B) it will bring them back to their younger years.

④ Most of this age group are suffering from one incurable illness or another, so fear of disease is not a big deterrent for them.

⑤ It will *really* tick off their kids.

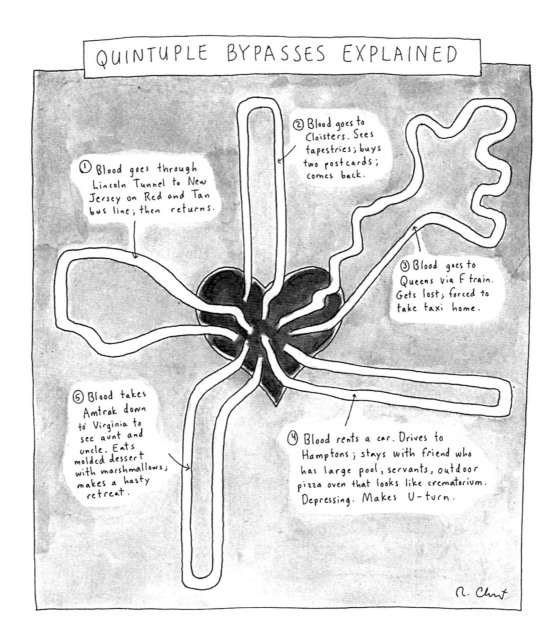

ROZ CHAST

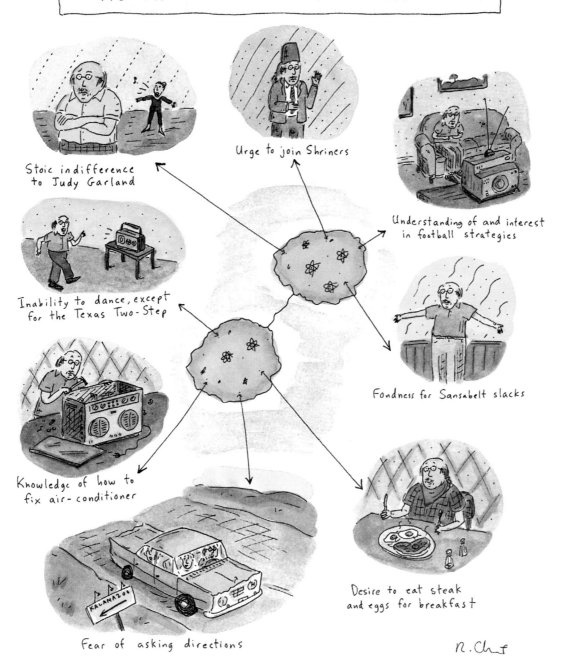

SCIENTISTS DISCOVER THE GENE FOR HETEROSEXUALITY IN MEN

Stoic indifference
to Judy Garland

Urge to join Shriners

Understanding of and interest
in football strategies

Inability to dance, except
for the Texas Two-Step

Fondness for Sansabelt slacks

Knowledge of how to
fix air-conditioner

Fear of asking directions

Desire to eat steak
and eggs for breakfast

R. Chast

THE GLASS FLOOR

ROZ CHAST

BIOLAB, INC.

GIGANTO® Avocados

Each weighs over one hundred pounds but must be used the same day it's opened.

HAWAIIAN HAM®

Pigs are cross-bred with pineapples and maraschino cherries to save today's busy cooks the fuss and bother of assembling all that stuff.

WATERMELETTES®

Golf ball-sized watermelons with edible rind. Perfect for snacks, lunchboxes, anytime.

SUPERHOT® Jalapeño Peppers

50,000,000 times as hot as regular Jalapeños. Cannot be used in any known recipe.

ALL-MEAT® Chicken

100% meat, through and through. No bones, no beak, no feet, no skin, no "icky parts." No waste – just chicken.

ALCOBROC®

One of nature's most nutritious vegetables – with an alcoholic content of 35%!

ROZ CHAST

WHEN BABY BOOMERS HIT THEIR NINETIES

Cataracts will become "cool."

There will be designer canes and walkers.

An entirely new type of cuisine will spring up as Mexican and Thai foods disappear from view.

Books about what it's like to be 100 will be major best-sellers.

ROZ CHAST

The Rites of Spring

How do the male and the female of the species perform the "mating dance"?

When the male wants the female's attention, he will probably puff up like a weather balloon.

EEAAAGH!!

Did I do something wrong?

Granted, this does not always work.

However, if the female **is** aroused, she will perform a display.

These are all of my shoes.

Either the male's attention will wander elsewhere ~

Are you listening to me?

or he will swing one or both of his arms around in a circular motion ~

doing what is known as "flailing" or "windmilling."

This behavior will continue until the female whacks him over the head with a stick.

What's the matter with you?!

Thus the courtship ritual is completed.

It'll be a June wedding!

And you're invited!

THEORIES OF EVERYTHING

ALTERNATIVE TREATMENTS for FAT MICE

Many mice have simply changed their wardrobes.

Some have found hypnosis to be a helpful dieting aid.

For others, liposuction is the only way to shed unwanted pounds.

For a long-term solution, however, most will have to revamp their life styles.

ROZ CHAST

OTHER REMBRANDT MISATTRIBUTIONS

Old Woman with Cellular Phone

Self-Portrait in Oversized-Brim Baseball Cap

View of Rotterdam

Young Girl at Her Bath

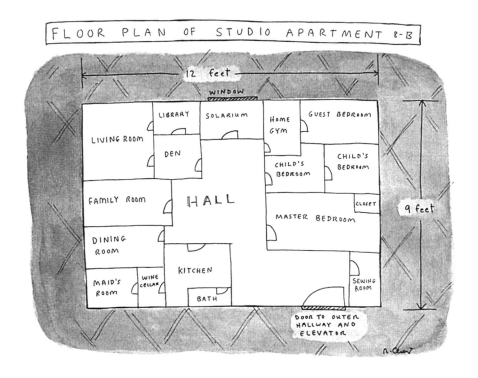

ROZ CHAST

WOODWORK. CLOTHES
FOR PEOPLE WHO WANT TO BLEND RIGHT IN

#329 Nondescript Shirt~
Put this on and no one will say, "Nice shirt!," "New?," or anything else, for that matter. Available in Pale and Quiet.

#470 Don't-Mind-Me Suit~
Do you want to look like everyone else? Then this is the suit for you. Comes in Nil, Efface, and Blah.

#638 Nothing-Special Skirt~
How many times have you wanted to just disappear completely? Order your skirt in Ignore, Vague, and Goodbye.

#855 Forgettable Raincoat~
Don't go to all the trouble of dressing to vanish and then blow it with your outer layer. Choose from Background or Sigh.

ROZ CHAST

THE DIALOGUES OF PLATO

Phrieda: Plato, what do you want for lunch?

Plato: Anything. Whatever.

Phrieda: How's tuna?

Plato: Not tuna.

Phrieda: I could make you some scrambled eggs.

Plato: Grilled cheese.

Phrieda: We don't have any cheese.

Plato: I want *grilled cheese!*

Phrieda: I'll go to the store later and buy some cheese, but <u>right</u> <u>now</u> <u>we</u> <u>don't</u> <u>have</u> <u>any</u> <u>cheese</u>, so tell me: *what do you want for lunch?*

Plato: I don't want anything.

Phrieda: You have to have something.

Plato: You can't force me.

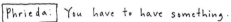

STOPPOS & SHOPPOS

r. ch

 CARDS

COLLECT THE ENTIRE SET!

#4: ESTHER J.

Ran out of orange juice one morning and served kids orange soda instead.

#17: GLORIA B.

Promised to take daughter to the mall after school— and then didn't.

#20: JAYNE R.

Sent child to school with 99.1°F. temperature - and child was sent home.

#23: LUCY L.

And then he...

Told friend "funny" story about kid and had a laugh at kid's expense.

#35: MARTINA F.

Didn't put up the St. Patrick's Day decorations one year.

#39: DAWN K.

When daughter left stuffed bear in Grand Union, waited until next day to retrieve it.

#48: SUZIE M.

Let kid play two hours of Nintendo— just to get him out of her hair.

#61: DEBORAH Z.

Has never even tried to make Play-Doh from scratch.

#89: BECKY O.

While on phone, told child to SHUT THE HELL UP, or she would brain her.

R. Chast

THEORIES OF EVERYTHING

THE BULL, THE BEAR, THE ANT, AND THE GRASSHOPPER

ROZ CHAST

THE WAGES OF SIN

ROZ CHAST

LESSER-KNOWN TENETS OF CREATIONISM

ROCKS

Rocks were originally animals that did something really, really bad.

PLANTS

Plants were rocks that did a good thing, like kept some important papers from blowing away, etc.

TREES

Trees suddenly appeared for no known reason. They are _not related_ to plants in ANY WAY WHATSOEVER.

ANIMALS

Animals were originally rocks that fell into a magic lake.

NOW AT THE ADULT POUND

Mitchell D. ~

Likes people, especially children. Very clean. Makes a good Tom Collins. Needs a loving home.

Gloria N. ~

Quiet. Good with plants. Not fussy about food or TV. Do you have room in your heart for her?

Lorraine S. ~

Mature but spry. Has had all her shots. Great for working couple.

Derek and Paula P. ~

Attractive and well-mannered duo. Knowledgeable about art, travel, fine wine - and yet still all alone in the world. Can you help?

UNUSUAL RETIREMENT PLANS

1000-F.A.I.

I'll take a thousand bucks, stick it in a bank, "forget about it," and in thirty years I'll be *pleasantly* surprised.

M.K. Plan

"My Kids" will take care of me. I'm virtually certain of that.

Jackpot Account

I'm not going to need one, because I'm going to be RICH, yessirree Bob.

The ? Plan

Who can plan, like, next week? Because an asteroid could smash into the Earth tomorrow, so what's the point?

THIS YEAR'S SPA

Picture yourself stretched out on a king-size tortilla, liberally sprinkled with nonfat cheese, olives, and chopped tomatoes, baking, baking, baking, until all your toxins are released.

$175

Relax on a twelve-grain wheatberry bun as we top you with organic pickles and ketchup. Then we'll place you under warming lights until every muscle unknots.

$250

First comes a Swedish massage. Then you'll be slathered with beaten eggs and rolled in fresh, homemade bread crumbs. Finally, you'll be "fried" in hot oil until your third eye opens.

$300

TOMORROW'S COSMIC REVELATIONS

The Universe is much, much wider than previously thought, but only half as tall.

There is an "up." Oddly enough, there is no "down."

Heaven has been positively located in the Upper Northeast Quadrant.

In addition to black and white holes, there are also orange, purple, and green holes. However, no one knows what they are for.

The Cosmos is 672 zeptoplillion years older than we used to think it was.

Cooking smells have been detected coming from Sector 53, but let us not jump to conclusions.

INTRODUCING...

THE 1040 - F.I.* FORM

* THE TAX RETURN FOR THE FINANCIALLY INCOMPETENT

① How much money do you guess you made last year?

☐ Under $10,000.

☐ Somewhere between $10,000 and $100,000.

☐ More than $100,000, but I don't know how or why.

② Did you save any receipts?

☐ I tried, but I just couldn't.

☐ I think there're some in a shoebox. I'll go look.

☐ No. What am I, an accountant?

③ Check payment preference.

☐ How could I owe anything? My year was lousy.

☐ Here's $15,000. If you need more, let me know.

☐ Blank check enclosed. You fill it in. Whatever.

ROZ CHAST

AN EXCERPT FROM
MEN ARE FROM BELGIUM, WOMEN ARE FROM NEW BRUNSWICK

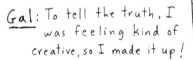

When women and men say:	They actually mean:
Guy: Is this meat loaf?	**Guy:** This is meat loaf, isn't it?
Gal: Of course it is, darling.	**Gal:** Do you have a problem with that?
Guy: Mmm. It's _delicious_!	**Guy:** It's awful.
Gal: I'm so glad you're enjoying it.	**Gal:** Isn't that a darn shame.
Guy: Did you use a recipe?	**Guy:** Did you just throw all this stuff together randomly, or what?
Gal: To tell the truth, I was feeling kind of creative, so I made it up!	**Gal:** So what if I did. SO WHAT. _SO, SO, SO WHAT!!!_
Guy: Next time, don't be shy about using a recipe, O.K.?	**Guy:** It's completely inedible, _that's_ what!
Gal: Okeydokey!	**Gal:** Your criticism stems from your own feelings of inadequacy. You should seek professional help.

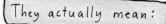

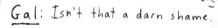

r. Chast

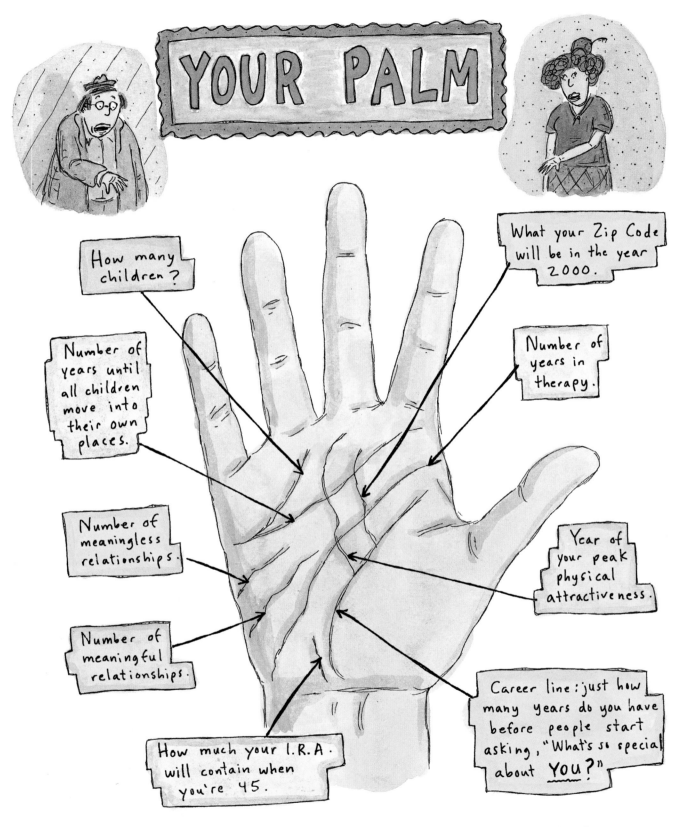

ROZ CHAST

ANGRY WHITE MALES
WHERE ARE THEY NOW?

CHARLES ADDAMS BY ROZ CHAST

When I was a kid, my parents and I used to escape the city and spend the summer up near Cornell University, in upstate New York.

Look! Trees!

Smell! Fresh air!

A whole contingent of Brooklyn schoolteachers went up there, to take courses and attend lectures – for, as my mother put it, "a certain degree of intellectualism."

This group included a barely five-foot-tall science teacher whose tan and extremely bald head was overflowing with plans of how to get free stuff from corporations...

I told them the pudding didn't jell and they sent me thirty boxes!

...a goateed, demonic-looking math teacher who was a compulsive punster and his pale, delicate wife with noticeably tiny feet...

Whatsamatter, you can't see the forest for the cheese?

...a social-studies teacher who wore clothes she designed herself, like the skirt with plastic pockets that held removable snapshots of all her friends....

Millie Davenport is OUT.

...and a Spanish teacher with a dime-size birthmark in the middle of his forehead, as well as countless others.

Anyway, on the Cornell campus was a browsing library. When my parents needed a little "intellectualism," they'd park me in there.

Okey-dokey!

Now, don't move a muscle till we get back!

There were no kids' books whatsoever, but there were *tons* of cartoon collections. I discovered Peter Arno, Helen Hokinson, George Price, Otto Soglow, and many more.

HUMOR

But the books I was obsessed with were by Charles Addams: <u>Monster Rally</u>, <u>Black Maria</u>, <u>Homebodies</u>, <u>Nightcrawlers</u>, <u>Drawn and Quartered</u>...I laughed at everything that I knew I shouldn't find funny: homicidal spouses; kids building guillotines in their rooms; and all those poor, unfortunate two-headed, three-legged, four-armed people.

Wolcott Gibbs, in his introduction to <u>Addams and Evil</u> wrote that Addams's work "is essentially a denial of all spiritual and physical evolution in the human race."

All in all, I'd have to agree.

Time to go!

Did you miss us?

TWO MORE POEMS from TED HUGHES

I once knew a lady from Mass.
Who was sometimes a pain in the ass.
Every damn comma
Was really high drama,
But she was quite a talented lass.

Sylvia Plath was my mate,
She and I went on a date.
She learned how to cook,
Then published a book,
And the rest is all up for debate.

THE MALE BIOLOGICAL CLOCK

If I don't learn how to play golf by the time I'm forty-three, I'll *never* learn.

ROZ CHAST

COME TAKE A JOURNEY TO THE ...

Have you ever stood at an airport baggage claim area and wondered what would eventually become of that sad, forlorn suitcase that kept going around and around?

Well, mostly, there are happy endings - tearful, emotion-packed reunions with rightful owners, etc.

Come to PAPA!

We were SO WORRIED!

You SCARED us!

We thought we'd NEVER SEE YOU AGAIN!

But what happens to that .0005 percent of bags that aren't so lucky? The ones that... _NEVER GET HOME?_

Uh oh.

Well, first they're held at the airport for five days... then, they're held in storage at another facility for about three months... and THEN... they get sent to...

Not me!

I'm RIGHT HERE!

Somebody COME GET ME!

They'll find me!

THE UNCLAIMED BAGGAGE CENTER...

(A TRUE STORY!)

No one's forgotten about ME...

... I hope!

...located in Scottsboro, Alabama, a tiny town in the northeast corner of the state. I had to go and see it for myself.

SCOTTSBORO

N.Y.C.

BIRMINGHAM

MONTGOMERY

For some idiotic reason, I had been expecting to run into hillbillies playing banjos and grandmas banging on triangles, calling the menfolk in for supper... DUH.

JETH-RO!

Instead, it was kind of empty ~ scrubby, flattish land with hills in the distance; billboards; interstates; and tons of churches.

LIFE IS SHORT- DEATH IS FOREVER.

GOD'S RETIREMENT HOME IS OUT OF THIS WORLD.

ACTUAL SIGNS

Finally, there it was ~ 33,000 square feet of lost luggage, and all of it for sale.

UNCLAIMED BAGGAGE CENTER

PLANET OF LOST LUGGAGE...

At first, it just seemed like the biggest second-hand store I'd ever set foot in...

...except for the fact that nobody had exactly voluntarily **DONATED** all this stuff.

Everything in this bag bores me.

Just one look at that rack of beige trenchcoats and you could hear three hundred Rabbit Angstroms, smacking their foreheads and saying, "Damn! I left my coat on the plane!"

But hey—finders keepers!

DANG!

There were racks and racks of skirts of all fabrics, patterns, styles, hues, and sizes...an entire carousel of white, freshly laundered, beautifully ironed men's shirts...sport jackets, leather jackets, windbreakers, and more.

Someone must have wondered about that suitcase full of saris...

...or this fetching belly-dancer's outfit...

BRA

ARM GIZMOS

SKIRT

ANKLE DEALS

BELT

...or a half-dozen brand-new tan shirts from an as yet unspecified "Department of Corrections," all size **EXTRA-LARGE**...

THERE WERE...

shoes

hats

party dresses

bathing suits

jogging suits

nightgowns

...even **UNDERWEAR.**

CON'T.

...IN SCOTTSBORO,

But it wasn't all clothes, NO SIRREE, BOB.

For instance, there was The Miracle Corner...

Praise the Lord!

I'm settin' my cane ASIDE!

... and an array of orphaned housewares.

I wonder what happened to that popcorn popper Aunt Gladys sent me.

POP KING

I spotted a basketful of wigs...

...and a crate of zippers...

The miscellaneous, half-used-up personal products shelf was thought-provoking...

FERRET CREAM RINSE

ANTI-VANDAL SPRAY

FOOT CARE

RIGHT GUARD

STRAINED PEAS

TALC

COLD CREAM

I wasn't sure that the bags of twenty or so previously owned tubes of toothpaste for two bucks were such a great deal...

There were over a thousand cameras. I imagined all the vacation photos that no one who wasn't in the photos would ever be forced to look at.

Someone had lost his Mega-Memory kit.

MEGA-MEMORY

American Memory Institute

EIGHT CASSETTES INSIDE

THE WORLD'S LARGEST MEMORY-TRAINING SCHOOL

Hope he didn't leave it on the plane.

I followed a lady in a sort of "romper-suit" for a while.

Maybe she was one of the locals who, I was told, came in two or three times a day.

Two o'clock! Time to check out the NEW MERCH!

ALABAMA!

I paid for the things I'd picked out:

CUFF-ETTES — *"the original translucent plastic sleeve protectors"

A long-wig-braid with great pictures on the package showing you different ways to attach it

3"→ 2"→

Pill-taking kit for the elderly — "My son bought this for me because he loves me" written on box

Tiny packet of rolled-up, disposable underpants from Japan

...and headed toward a lunch counter nearby that I'd heard served regional fare.

LUNCH

The place was empty. I sat at the counter and ordered a "peanut coke," just out of curiosity.

The waitress balefully went behind the counter and extracted this big, dingy plastic tub containing about an inch of old-looking peanuts. She spooned them into the coke.

They drifted down.

Then they floated up again.

Then they drifted down. It was like watching a lava lamp.

When I tried to drink it, the peanuts got stuck in the straw.

I poked around Scottsboro some more.

THE PRISSY HEN — TU-LU'S NEEDFUL THINGS FOR LADIES — THE DIABETES SHOPPE

← ACTUAL STORE NAMES

What else was it like? Well, if you were down on your luck, you could buy a two-bedroom house with a "privacy fence" for $30,000...

...but if things were looking up, $250,000 would buy you a 3600 square foot extravaganza on 38 acres, plus an inground pool.

The closest I came to hillbillies was the Brunswick Stew ($24.50 a gallon) at the local barbecue joint, which apparently is made out of squirrels.

BRUNSWICK STEW — PURE SQUIRREL GOODNESS IN EVERY BITE!

I didn't try it.

I went to the Ave Maria Grotto where an obsessed hunchbacked monk made 135 miniature shrines out of marbles, cement, seashells, glass, bathroom tiles, and whatever else was handy.

LOURDES, FRANCE

I never got to "Nixon's Chapel," a nearby town...

...or "A Touch of German," a store with a Tyrolean fixation.

Ja!

On the way home, I thought about what the Unclaimed Baggage press kit had said: "It is not the baggage, but the **owner** who is lost, because the baggage is actually in hand in Scottsboro." And in a way, I had to admit they were right.

ROZ CHAST

BETTY ANN IN CANNES

Last night, I had the strangest dream: I'd won three tickets to the Cannes Film Festival.

The only stipulation was I had to go with my parents.

It's not like I have this huge bone to pick with them. It's just that... well, NEVER MIND.

Anyway, we're walking along the Riviera. It's incredibly beautiful.

We are surrounded by all these gorgeous people.

ASTONISHING   ALARMINGLY PERFECT   A COMPLETELY OTHER SPECIES

For some reason, the three of us are still lugging around our suitcases...

Everyone looks relaxed and happy to be there...

except, of course, US.

Your father is hungry.

No, it can wait.

It's LUNCH-TIME.

We find this grungy little diner and sit at the counter, even though we're the only ones in the place.

At the end of the meal, there's some big disagreement about the check.

I did NOT order the "de-luxe" tuna platter.

By the time it's all straightened out, we've missed the festival.

We showed HIM who's boss!

THEORIES OF EVERYTHING

GIFTS FROM THE
HOUSE OF LOW GOALS

T-Shirts

Special-Occasion Cakes

Cards

Trophies

ROZ CHAST

A MARTHA STEWART MOMENT IN APARTMENT 8-J

ROZ CHAST

ROZ CHAST

INSIDE ONE'S MEMORY BANK

By the time you're forty, all available drawers are completely filled.

You learn something new, something else gets thrown out.

People think they can get around this by cramming stuff into already-in-use drawers, but they're sadly mistaken.

And in the end everything turns into material whose only function is to keep one's head from collapsing in on itself.

DESCENT INTO THE MAELSTROM

SIX HOURS IN THE CAR WITH...

 DAD

 MOM

 TIMMY

 JUDY

HOUR ONE

JUDY: I'm hungry.

MOM: How can you be hungry? We just left the house.

TIMMY: I'm cold.

DAD: You're not cold. It's 90° outside.

JUDY: Are we there yet?

HOUR TWO

DAD: Whoever sees an animal first gets 50¢.

JUDY: Look! There's a bug on the windshield! I get 50¢!

TIMMY: That's not an _animal_, that's an _insect_, you dork.

JUDY: Insects _ARE_ animals, jerk.

TIMMY: But that doesn't mean they _COUNT_.

JUDY: Dad? Do insects count?

MOM: Why don't we all enjoy this beautiful scenery?

HOUR THREE

TIMMY: Leave me alone.

JUDY: What am I _DOING???_

TIMMY: Your foot just touched my foot.

MOM: You guys are not allowed to _look_ at each other, _speak_ to each other, or _touch_ each other. _IS THAT CLEAR???_

TIMMY: (something under breath.)

JUDY: MOM!!!!!

HOUR FOUR

DAD: IF THERE IS ANY MORE NONSENSE FROM BACK THERE, I WILL PULL OVER AND SPANK YOU BOTH TILL YOU SEE STARS! SO HELP _ME_ GOD!! THE END!!!!!

MOM: Look at that old barn over there.

HOUR FIVE

TIMMY: Guess what? We haven't had our seat belts on this _whole_ time!

MOM AND DAD: PUT YOUR SEAT BELTS ON RIGHT THIS MINUTE!

HOUR SIX

TIMMY: Let's play Smashies.

JUDY: What's Smashies?

TIMMY: It's when you put your hand on top of the cooler and I try to smash it.

JUDY: Like this?

TIMMY: (SMASH)

JUDY: _OW!_ That hurt!

TIMMY: Wanna play Pinchies?

MOM: Does anybody want some grapes?

r. Chr

THIS SPRING, TRY...
LIFE'S END.
CLOTHING FOR PEOPLE WHO HAVE JUST GIVEN UP

#103~ Super-Duper Cozy Zip-locked Sleepwear
Because, let's face it: who wants somebody messing with them just as they're going to sleep?

#275~ Unattractive-Length Skirt
Scientists in our lab have worked for years to determine exactly the most repellent length for a skirt ~ and here it is!

#399~ Way Negative-Heel Shoes
If a high heel makes a woman look _more_ desirable, what do you think its _opposite_ does?

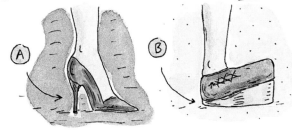

#192~ Comatose-Fit Jeans
To hell with "relaxed." Let's get real.

#316~ Fanny Pack
Strap on one of these and watch women turn aside in disgust.

I can't look.

#487~ Life's End. Swim Garments
Don't you wish _everyone_ wore one?

ROZ CHAST

THE N.R.A.'s WRITTEN TEST FOR A GUN LICENSE

① My favorite kind of gun is a _____, because _____.

② When I carry a gun, I feel _____, and the bigger the gun the more _____ I feel.

③ My favorite part of shooting is when _____ _____ _____,

④ If a robber tried to rob me, I'd shoot him in the _____.

⑤ In my fantasies, the three people I'd most like to blow away are _____, _____, and _____.

⑥ Guns are like rolls of Scotch tape. There should be at least ___ in every room of the house.

⑦ I'm all for gun safety, but _____ _____ _____ _____ _____.(Use reverse side if necessary.)

⑧ People who don't like guns are _____ and ought to be _____.

THE ANCIENT TEA CEREMONY of ASTORIA

① THE FILLING OF THE SACRED VESSEL

② THE PLACING OF THE VESSEL UPON THE FIRE

③ THE SOUNDING OF THE WHISTLE OF BOILOSITY

④ THE DECANTING INTO THE CEREMONIAL MUG

⑤ THE HOLY STEEPING OF THE TEA BAG

⑥ THE MYSTICAL SAVING OF THE TEA BAG FOR FUTURE USE

R. Chast

ROZ CHAST

REALTOR FROM THE BLACK LAGOON

"OH, YOU *REALLY* SHOULDN'T HAVE" HOLIDAY GIFTS

ANTI-AGING CREME SAMPLER

Your loved one will be speechless with gratitude.

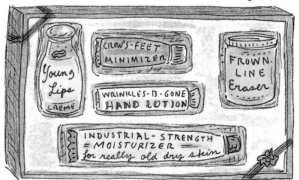

Young Lips CREME

CROW'S-FEET MINIMIZER

WRINKLES-B-GONE HAND LOTION

FROWN-LINE Eraser

INDUSTRIAL-STRENGTH MOISTURIZER for really old dry skin

DIETER'S ASSORTMENT PAK

Your paramour won't know how to thank you.

LET'S COUNT CALORIES! 50? 30? 950? 275? 150? 27? 10?

Sugarless Candies

GYM MEMBERSHIP CARD

BODY-FAT PERCENTAGE CALIPERS

PERSONAL HYGIENE MEDLEY

Anyone who receives this will wonder at your thoughtfulness.

FILM-AWAY TOOTHPASTE

FLOSS

SMELL GUARD JUMBO ECONOMY SIZE

EXTRA-HEAVY-DUTY MOUTH-WASH

SOAP

LOVE LIFE IMPROVEMENT KIT

He or she will be moved to tears.

MALE & FEMALE ANATOMY: A PULL-OUT GUIDE

VHS Let's Get Out of Our Rut! 120 MINUTES

MARTINIS ONE QUART

R. Chast

FOR THEIR OWN GOOD

It isn't that difficult to shield children from death.

Mommy? Where's Grandpa?

With a little ingenuity, you can keep them in the dark for 15, 16 years—or even more.

Huh?

LIFE IS A MYSTERY
IN YOUR TIME OF SORROW
Our Prayers Are with You
TEARS
SORROW
CONDOLENCES
WITH SYMPATHY
SYMPATHY
ACME COLLEGE

We'll start with an easy one: you're watching Bambi, and Bambi's mom gets shot.

FWAKK

Simply look her in the eye and say:

She's fine! I saw her LAST WEEK!! In the woods behind GRAND UNION!!!

Let's say he or she gets curious about cemeteries:

It's a STONE STORE.

Pet death? Watch and learn:

What's wrong with Fifi?

Quick! Look over there.

Do the old switcheroo—

HURL

What? Where? I don't see anything.

—and it's like nothing ever happened.

Fifi had brown stripes.

No, she didn't.

MEOW

Why not keep it on a "need to know" basis? After all—who needs to know?

Grandpa is in the Belgian Congo.

ROZ CHAST

ROZ CHAST

UNCHARTED WATERS

I learned to sail seven years ago.

Make a right. NO! NOT A LEFT!! A RIGHT!!!

I spent all my time in the harbor, just doing what needed to be done.

It was boring but safe. I always knew where I was.

I could maneuver my craft reasonably well.

That counts me out.

I even had all the sailor's knots down cold.

"KRENSKY'S KONUNDRUM"

"WHIFFENPOOF"

"HER MAJESTY"

"THE BUZZARD"

Finally, there came a day when it was time to take her out to the open sea.

At first, the limitless expanse of sea and sky was exhilarating.

I'm FREE!

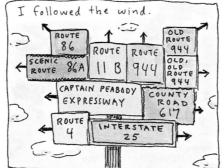

I followed the wind.

But as the shoreline receded I realized I was getting farther and farther from home.

Uh-oh.

The air was turning cooler. I could sense a storm approaching.

I don't know where the ★@#%. I am.

Using all my concentration, I steered her back to the safety of the harbor.

Thank God!

Still and all, for a first trip, it wasn't a complete failure.

THEORIES OF EVERYTHING

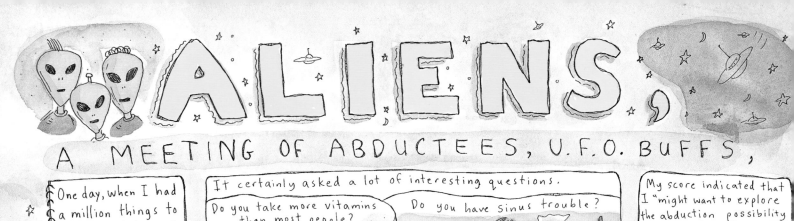

ALIENS,

A MEETING OF ABDUCTEES, U.F.O. BUFFS,

One day, when I had a million things to do, but didn't want to do any of them, I took a "Have You Ever Been Abducted by Aliens?" test.

It certainly asked a lot of interesting questions.

Do you take more vitamins than most people?

Do you have sinus trouble?

Do you ever have insomnia?

Do you ever have flying dreams?

Do you secretly feel you are special?

Well, maybe a little...

My score indicated that I "might want to explore the abduction possibility further."

So, on a cold and rainy day last spring, I attended an all-day conference on alien abduction held in a church in Boston.

ALIEN CONFERENCE TODAY 9 A.M.—6:30 P.M.

Speakers would include an Alien Abduction Expert; a Brazilian shaman; a Native American; a couple of local "experiencers" (what those in the know call abductees; an ex-astronaut; some "Western Scientists"; and a few other alien aficionados.

I checked out the crowd. Plenty of shawls, dangly earrings, and peasant-y handbags, but mostly Averages Joes and Janes.

There were, of course, a few bonafide eccentrics.

Feather tied around head with string

Guy with 90° angled hair and beard

My favorites were the guys who looked like photos of the authors of the U.F.O. books I always read as a child.

"Official" badge from U.F.O. institute

Overweight, beard, glasses

Many pens in pocket protector

The Native American guy, who resembled Johnny Cash, worked the crowd by walking around and fanning us with smoke from a dish of incense.

The Alien Expert began the morning's lecture by describing a typical abduction scenario:

You're in your car or home. There's a bright light, humming. Maybe you feel some anxiety...

...you see one or more aliens...

Uh oh.

Then you're floated through walls, through a roof... Experiencers will often say, "every cell is vibrating... my body is coming apart."

SPLINK

AHOY!

AND THE CURIOUS: A TRUE STORY

Then you're taken onto a craft where a doctor-like being probes you, taking sperm or eggs to make hybrids...

This does not bode well...

...On subsequent visits, you'll be asked to nurture these offspring...

DAD, GIVE KEYS TO CAR, DAD.

Thought telepathically communicated

...And if you're lucky, you'll get to meet your alien mate.

Then the shaman told his story: He was on a riverbank in Brazil...

La, la, la-

when suddenly, "three small humanoids in aluminum costumes" emerged from a U.F.O. which had just landed nearby.

He felt his body disintegrate. The next thing he knew, he was back on the riverbank, but he had healing powers.

Cool!

DZZT

DZZT

Next, we heard from "Johnny Cash." He was in a garden, when a spaceship appeared.

What the—

He was beamed aboard the ship, which took him to a planet where the buildings were pure white and luminous.

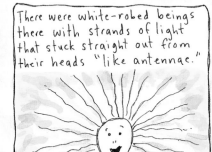

There were white-robed beings there with strands of light that stuck straight out from their heads "like antennae."

He liked the aliens. He'd been a drug addict and had done time, and he felt that they were helping him to understand all that.

They offered him a chance to stay, but when he realized that by staying, he'd lose "his **house**, his **car**, and his **family**," he decided to return to Earth.

No way— I'm **OUTTA** here!

SOB!

Then came the two local experiencers.

The first one began his story:

I have been on their tables... I have been on their ships... I have been a part of that blue light...

Whatever had happened to this guy had made him *pretty upset.*

CON'T.

When the Big Blues are there, everything's fine. But then the Little Grays come out, and it's NOT fine...

There were little ones with BIG EYES and NO HEARTS that do things that AREN'T VERY NICE!!!

The other guy seemed more at peace with the whole thing.

They're benevolent... ...I think.

Then it was lunchtime. I had signed up for the only thing they offered: the vegetarian box lunch.

↑ cold, rolled-up vegetable and grain mush

↑ world's worst brownie made from a microwave mix

It cost ten bucks.

But before we ate, I had a close encounter of my own: I ran into someone I hadn't seen in years. I asked him what he'd been up to, and he told me a very strange story:

"I was traveling in South America and met up with some indigenous tribesmen...

Hello!

I was interested in the consciousness-expanding drugs of the region. They gave me an herb called 'Iawatty' which they brewed in a tea...

As it took effect, I felt an alien intelligence scan my entire body from head to toe...

It stopped at my left knee. I couldn't figure out why. Then, I remembered an old skiing injury, and realized it was trying to under-stand scar tissue...

??? ???

It finished its scan. I felt my 'self' leave my body... I was floating...

WHEEE!

Suddenly, a loud disembodied voice boomed out:

SYSTEM FAILURE!!!
SYSTEM FAILURE!!!
CELLULAR MEMORY!!!
CELLULAR MEMORY!!!

I was frightened. My consciousness had gone to a place before there were cells. Now I had to return to my body~ OR DIE.

My guides brought me back and I was fine."

I was happy it had all worked out o.k. for him and wished him well.

 I got my lunch and sat at a table in a big room that had been set up for us.

 My tablemate, a psychiatric nurse, was telling her friend about a patient who thought he had an alien implant in his ear, and how she believed him 100 percent.

Even if it had shown up on the X-ray, the doctors would probably have thrown it away, she said.

Seen one, seen 'em all.

 There was lots of "abductee wannabee" talk:

As far as I know, I'm not an experiencer.

If I was abducted, and maybe I was, I don't know...

OVERHEARD IN PASSING

H-E-E-E-ERE!

BY ROZ CHAST, WHO DID NOT MAKE ANY OF THIS UP.

After lunch, the "Western Scientists" spoke. An ex-astronaut and an astrophysicist discussed quantum physics and other stuff that was way over my head.

$E=mc^2$

A "Remote Viewing Instructor and Director of Inner Vision in Las Vegas" explained how she had stumbled upon her abductee past while watching a slide show about alien abduction, and explained her philosophy.

A lot of scientists — I won't say all — read tarot cards, are into numerology, and study runes.

This was news to me, but *whatever.*

Finally, it was time for our Afternoon Workshops. We all headed off for our separate groups that met in the church's smaller rooms on the second floor.

I got into the Healing Workshop! How about you?

"Exercises for Enhancing Altered State Perception"!

Mine was "The Transformative Journey," led by the Alien Abduction Expert himself.

The Expert started things off by getting us in the right mood.

Has anything in this conference today *stirred up anything?*

I felt as if I were sitting around a campfire when someone announced he was going to tell a really, really spooky story.

OOOOOOOHHHOOOOOOHH

He asked if any of us were "experiencers," and nearly half of the thirty people in the room raised their hands.

One by one, people told their stories. Some were pretty intriguing.

...so they put their baby on my chest. I said, "this is very strange." Then...

I met a beautiful woman and felt ecstasy.

There were blondes, brunettes...they had an *oriental* quality.

But others... it was a mystery.

Since my abduction, I am sensitive to electro-magnetic fields.

They're coming back for me, but I DON'T KNOW WHEN!

Is there a support group for people who worry about spontaneous combustion?

The fact was, I'd never seen a U.F.O., but I knew some relatively sane people who had. Who could say what the real deal was?

On the way out, I bought a souvenir: a serious-looking 683-page textbook about Alien Abduction:

ALIEN TYPES: BUMBLING ALIENS, PAGE 30
#@#*!!!
"..." KNOCK

ALIEN PROCEDURES: REMOVE AND PUT BACK TOP OF HEAD, PAGE 57
A. B.

CAMERAS TO DETECT ALIENS: MAY CUT DOWN ON VISITS, PAGE 472

This'll fix 'em!

REAL! DECIDING WHAT IS OR ISN'T, PAGE 82

A couple of weeks later, I visited an alien-implant removal website. It said, if I called this number: 707-527-5700, I'd find out:
① how many times I'd been abducted, and —
② how many implants I had.

Don't ask me why, but I chickened out.

R. Chast

HOME SCHOOLING

Math
Go to the grocery store with ten bucks. Buy milk, bread, a pack of Tareytons, and a TV Guide. Make sure you return with the right change.

Science
The venetian blinds are grimy. Experiment till you find the best way to get them clean.

Social Studies
Leave the house for a couple of hours and observe people.

English
Go to your room and read for as long as you like.

GEORGE GERSHWIN, PSYCHIATRIST

ROZ CHAST

ONE MORNING, WHILE GETTING DRESSED,

YOU

DON'T EXAMINE THE LABEL OF YOUR SHIRT

EXAMINE THE LABEL OF YOUR SHIRT

AND PUT IT ON

AND SEE THAT IT'S MADE IN

AND FORGET ABOUT IT

MEXICO

THAILAND

THE U.S.

AND REALIZE THAT THE PEOPLE WHO MADE YOUR SHIRT

PROBABLY HAVE DYSENTERY OR DIPHTHERIA OR WORSE

EARNED THREE CENTS AN HOUR

HATE YOUR STUPID YANKEE GUTS

ROZ CHAST

Price $3.00

Nov. 22, 1999

THE NEW YORKER

THEORIES OF EVERYTHING

When in Rome...

The whole time I lived in Brooklyn, I never *once* thought about napkin folding.

crack-head

crack store

crack vials

Connecticut was a different story.

We're having the mudroom repapered in Tunisian silk next week. Then we have to install the pneumatic shingling and the terra-cotta bruschetta oven.

One day I decided to check out the natives.

BMW FOR SALE · DOG WALKING · POOL CLEANING · NAPKIN-FOLDING SEMINAR · REGISTER NOW! · CAT LOST · YARD WORK · A.A. MEETING

I tried to blend in.

Would you ladies like to learn how to fold a napkin?

Apparently, no one had a job.

We'll start with a Bishop's Hat.

Did no one else find this peculiar?

First, you fold it so it looks like a boat.

Who *were* all these people?

Then you peel this back. Then you flip it over and tuck in this piece.

Had they all just crash-landed from Planet Eisenhower??

Then you line it up just *so.*

WHO WERE THEY KIDDING???

Then I stick my hand in...

Then again, they were probably all very nice folks...

...and flip it over and peel these back.

...nice, sensible, responsible, God-fearing, upstanding, solid citizens.

Then you stick a doodad on it, and *voilà!*

The minute the kids leave for college, we're moving back to the city.

Now, who's ready for the accordion fold?

SIGH

THEORIES OF EVERYTHING

DECONSTRUCTING LUNCH

① IT'S A SANDWICH:
That, in itself, means you are a *normal* child from a *normal* family.

② IT'S ON WHOLE-WHEAT BREAD:
O.K., so we're liberal, big-city Democrats.

③ BUT IT'S THE BIG-BRAND, EASY-TO-CHEW KIND:
I didn't say "radical." I said "liberal."

④ BOLOGNA AND MAYO:
People *always* mistake us for Republicans!

⑤ IT'S KOSHER BOLOGNA:
It's not about religion—it's about *taste*.

⑥ LETTUCE:
Other parents may not care about their kids' health, but *I* do.

⑦ LOOK, THERE'S A SLICE OF AMERICAN CHEESE IN THERE:
If you want to become a Mormon, I'll love you anyway. I just want you to be happy.

ROZ CHAST

FRED PHILPOT
BORN 1944

LET IT ALL
HANG OUT
1967 – 1979

STUFFED IT ALL
BACK IN
1980 – 2007

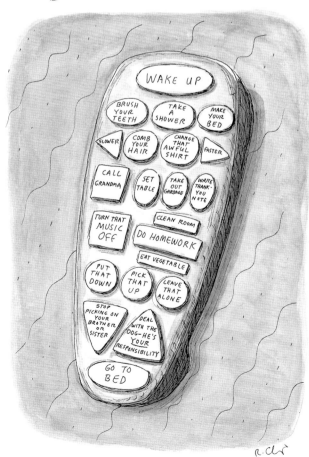

THE DREAM REMOTE

PUBLIC TV's "REALITY" SHOWS

Modern Dance Bloopers

When Good Mathematicians Go Bad

I'll just make something up over here.

Who Wants to Marry a College Graduate with a Liberal Arts Degree?

BEHIND CLOSED DOORS

APEXCO

Pencil Sharpening	1ST fl.
Sorting	2nd fl.
Rumor Mongering	3rd fl.
Apple Polishing	4th fl.
On Hold	5th fl.
Coffee Brewing	6th fl.
Looking Out Window	7th fl.
Internet Browsing	8th fl.
Gloating	PH

ROZ CHAST

THE DOWNWARD SPIRAL

THEORIES OF EVERYTHING

EXTREMELY PRACTICAL JOKES

Joy of Health Buzzer

Ask to shake someone's hand. If the person's cholesterol is too high, the device will buzz. A real lifesaver.

Trick Vitamin Gum

Tastes just like ordinary gum — but it's packed with vitamins!

Whoopee Posture Cushion

Think about it: why would you say "WHOOPEE!" if you sat on a pillow that made an embarrassing noise?

Dental X-Ray Specs

A moment's laughter? Or eternal gratitude? It's your choice.

PASSIVE-AGGRESSIVE BIRTHDAY GIFTS

"FOR WHEN YOU DON'T LIKE THE KID... OR THE PARENTS"

THE LAST FAMILY VACATION

HOW THE OLD PENN STATION GOT DEMOLISHED

ROZ CHAST

FOOD WARS
"THE THRILLA IN PEEKSKILLA"

ROZ CHAST

ITEM # 3715 - COZY CARDIGAN

Snuggle up in this oh-so-cozy cardigan.
Once you slip it on, you'll never want to
take it off. We've improved the fit and the
texture ~ it's a hug made of wool, a hug that
never lets go before you're ready to be let go. Whether
you're just sitting at home with your family, who must
think you're some kind of automaton and take you for
granted day in and day out, who can't be bothered to clean
up after themselves, it's a wonder you're not a complete
alcoholic, or whether you're going to work at the widget office where all
day long, you have the privilege of watching your boss making goo-goo
eyes at that thing in the black leather miniskirt that a normal person with
her legs would never wear, and finally it's five o'clock and you can go
home to your empty apartment overlooking two gas stations and a
restaurant that is probably a Mafia money-laundering operation
because it has all this expensive but ugly junk in it and about
seven waiters per customer because no one ever
eats there, and you wonder: is this all there is?,
this is the sweater you'll reach for over
and over again. We guarantee it!

Black, white, red, green, navy........ S, M, L, XL - $39.95

R. Chast

ROZ CHAST

ROZ CHAST

THE NEW CAR

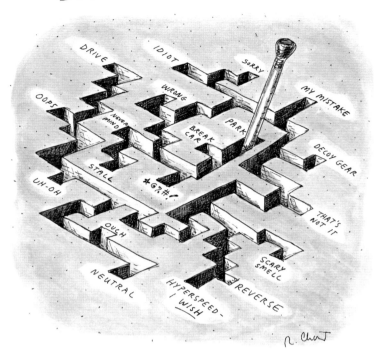

THE VAIN BUT REALISTIC QUEEN

ROZ CHAST

TRUE CONFESSIONS

ROZ CHAST

SPRING CLEANING

If the mate to a sock has not reappeared in three years, put it in a box marked "SINGLE SOCKS" and forget about it.

Spend nine hours meticulously going over a toaster with a non-abrasive cleaner, vinegar, soap and water, a toothbrush, paper towels, and Q-tips until it's PERFECT.

Take all your books off the shelves. Go through them. Then put them all back.

> I remember this one!

It is a law of nature that even if a toy has not been played with in <u>ten years</u>, if you throw it out, its absence WILL BE NOTICED.

> Ma, I can't find GREEN BEAR.

When all is said and done, take a deep breath and get rid of <u>one</u> knick-knack.

R. Chst

MIXED MARRIAGE

EPISODE 3: "IRREGARDLESS"

JESUS! Did you hear that?

No. What?

That newscaster just said "IRREGARDLESS"!

So?

Doesn't that bother you?

No - why should it?

Well, I happen to think that newscasters should KNOW THE CORRECT WORD, THAT'S ALL!!!

What's it supposed to be, "disregardless"?

All I'm saying is that people who say "irregardless" are TOTAL CRETINS!

LOTS of people say "irregardless."

That's exactly my point! "LOTS" of people ARE cretins!!!

Look: just because a person doesn't have "BOOK SMARTS" doesn't mean he or she is STUPID!

That newscaster might have a lot of EMOTIONAL intelligence!

May I interject one teensy-weensy thought?

Go ahead!

Emotional intelligence is CRAP!!!

ROZ CHAST

SURROUNDSOUND

THE SEDER PLATE AT YE OLDE YANKEE INNE

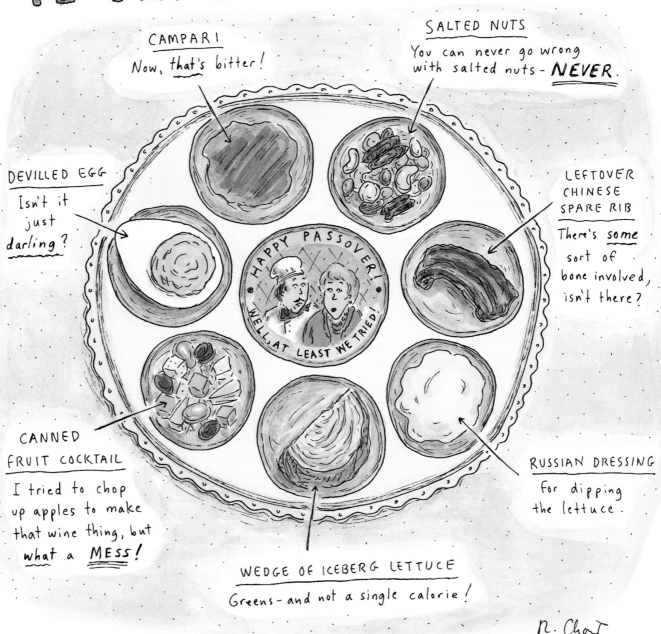

CAMPARI
Now, *that's* bitter!

SALTED NUTS
You can never go wrong with salted nuts — <u>NEVER</u>.

DEVILLED EGG
Isn't it just darling?

LEFTOVER CHINESE SPARE RIB
There's <u>some</u> sort of bone involved, isn't there?

HAPPY PASSOVER!
WELL, AT LEAST WE TRIED!

CANNED FRUIT COCKTAIL
I tried to chop up apples to make that wine thing, but what a <u>MESS</u>!

WEDGE OF ICEBERG LETTUCE
Greens — and not a single calorie!

RUSSIAN DRESSING
For dipping the lettuce.

R. Chast

ROZ CHAST

ADMISSIONS TEST FOR THE DANBURY INSTITUTE OF PHILOSOPHY

1. How many minutes a day do you spend thinking?
☐ two or fewer ☐ fifteen ☐ a billion

2. Are your thoughts:
☐ like a slow, orderly procession of elephants, or...
☐ like rabbits chasing each other in circles, or...
☐ like gnats?

3. What are your thoughts mostly about?
☐ sex in the year 3000   ☐ parallel parking
☐ mealtime   ☐ illness and death
☐ getting back at people   ☐ real estate

4. Which outward signs usually accompany your thinking (check any that apply)?
☐ wrinkled forehead   ☐ index finger pointing to temple
☐ tongue protruding from mouth   ☐ hair standing on end

MAIL COMPLETED FORM TO:

Plato Jones
Suite 410
Danbury Industrial Tower and Rotunda
Danbury, New York

BOUTIQUE GASOLINES

CHÂTEAU HAUT-SUNOCO 1985

"A fleshy yet powerful blend, with notes of oak, pepper, coffee, and chocolate."

~ Ed, *The Gasoline Spectator*

TEXACO CLASSICO 1992

"A fuel of purity and symmetry, revealing a heady aroma of black cherry, licorice, and leather."

~ Gus, *Gasoline Enthusiast*

Domaine de Mobil 1997

"Drivers will enjoy its exotic nose of coconut, plums, and fresh-cut grass."

~ Dwayne, *Gas and Oil Connoisseur*

THE BOOK OF MILLIE

And lo, Millie looked into the mirror and beheld her thighs, and cried unto the Lord, "Oh, Lord! Whatst shall I do with these stupid thighs that are like massive tree trunks?" And the Lord said, "She that believeth in me shall have thighs of great slenderness everlastingly."

BEFORE   AFTER

ROZ CHAST

INACUPRESSURE POINTS

OUCH.

QUIT IT.

THIS ISN'T HELPING AT ALL.

WILL YOU PLEASE STOP?

NO.

LEAVE THAT ALONE.

CHUCK YOU, FARLEY.

STOP TOUCHING ME.

CUT THAT OUT.

DON'T.

UNCLE.

A LOOK AHEAD

36% - SORT OF A MISHMASH

9% - SWIFT AND MERCIFUL

14% - QUICK BUT EXCRUCIATING

26% - DRAWN-OUT BUT PRETTY COMFORTABLE

15% - LONG AND PAINFUL

CLOUD CHART

LONERS

Single clouds that like to hang out in an otherwise cloudless sky.

SHEEP

Little clouds that always appear in bunches.

SPEEDY GONZALI

Clouds in a huge hurry to get to the next sky.

BLOCKERS

Mischievous clouds with a fondness for popping up just as one decides to go in the ocean.

GRAY BLANKET

One vast gray cloud that usually covers several states at once.

INDUSTRIOS

Beautiful clouds that are most often seen over large manufacturing plants.

SIGMUNDS

Clouds with an uncanny ability to make you feel anxious or depressed.

DUHS

No-name, generic clouds having no meteorological significance whatsoever.

R. Chast

ROZ CHAST

TOUR OF CATHEDRAL #4,019

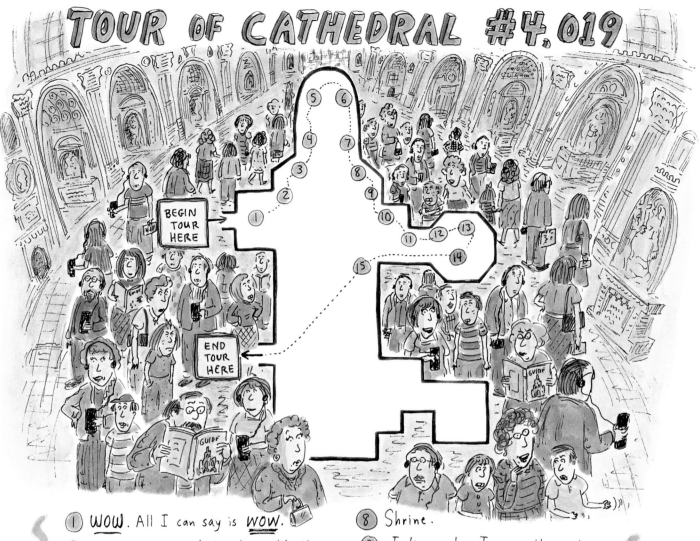

BEGIN TOUR HERE

END TOUR HERE

① WOW. All I can say is WOW.

② How did they build structures like this without modern machinery? It's AMAZING!!!

③ Look at that _beautiful_ _stained_ _glass!_ I am in AWE.

④ The _bottom of my shoe_ is actually touching a stone that somebody put here in maybe 1200 A.D.

⑤ Wish I hadn't worn these **specific** shoes, though. Oh, well.

⑥ This really is incredible.

⑦ How was I supposed to know that that old chair was part of the exhibit???

⑧ Shrine.

⑨ I _knew_ when I wore these shoes that they were uncomfortable, but I wore them **anyway**. I DESERVE to suffer.

⑩ I think I'm getting hungry.

⑪ More stained glass.

⑫ How can I be hungry? I just had breakfast two hours ago!

⑬ Yes, but it was very unsatisfying.

⑭ There is _no way_ I'm as fat as that lady.

⑮ Exit: yesssss!

ROZ CHAST

DOG DAY

ROZ CHAST

ROZ CHAST

NEWLY DISCOVERED LEARNING DISABILITIES

GO-CARTITIS

Instead of focussing on topic at hand, kid fantasizes about go-carts.

DOODLER'S SYNDROME

Child insists on drawing, thus completely shutting out teacher's voice.

CLOCK-WATCHING DISORDER

He or she plays mental games with wall clock rather than pay full attention.

JIMMY'S CONDITION

Student gets on own train of thought, and that is the end of THAT.

ROZ CHAST

The Final Chapter

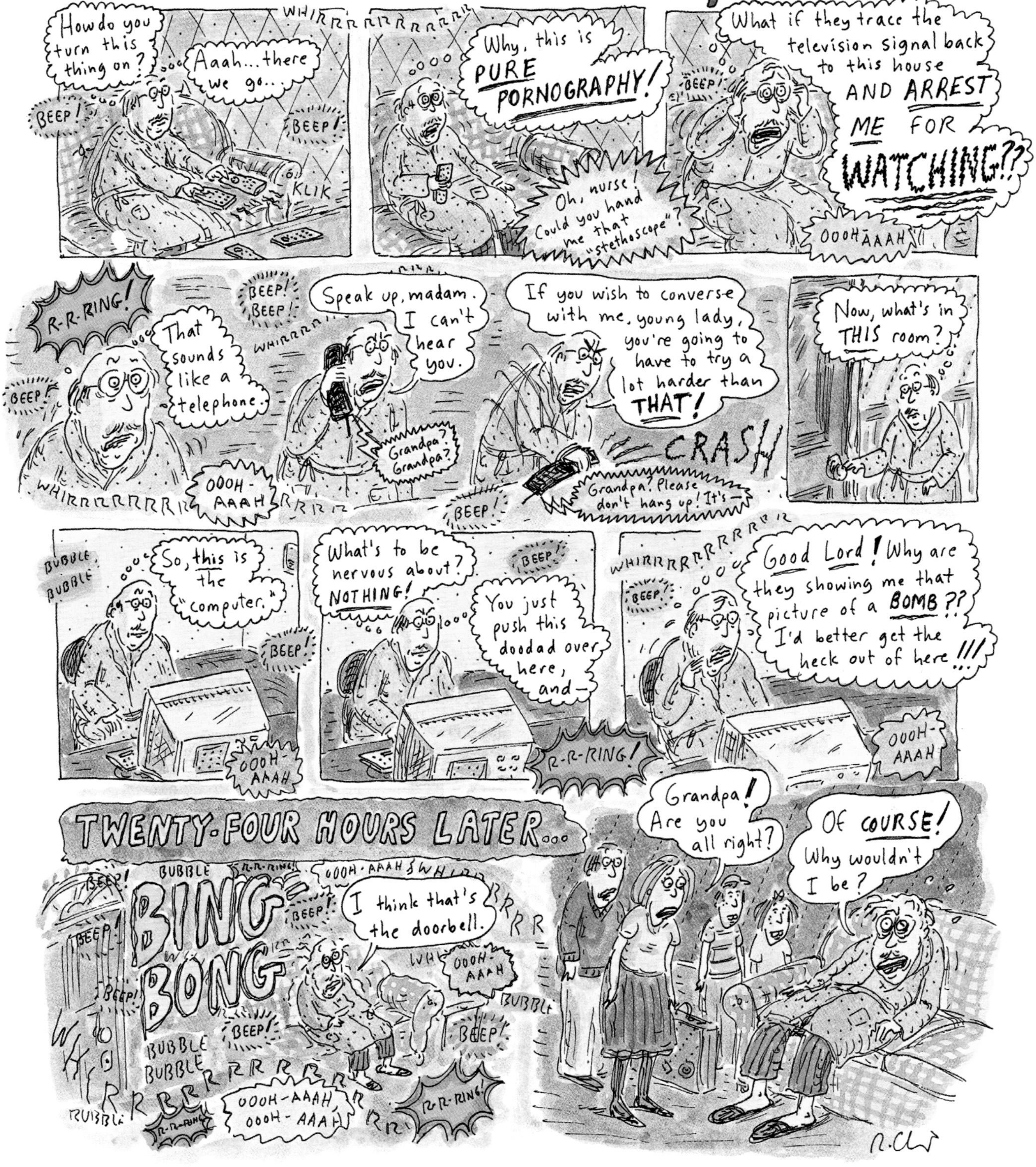

TV FOR ONE
SITCOMS FOR THE NON-SOCIAL

One of a Kind

Show about a gal who minds her own beeswax, with hilarious results.

Me, Myself, and I

Laughfest about a guy who doesn't quite see the point of "relationships."

Just Us Chickens

Thirty minutes of sidesplitting comedy as a young woman keeps to herself.

Single Serving Size

You'll love this new mirth-'plosion about a fellow who is tired of dealing with others.

R. Chst

ROZ CHAST

STRANGE WRESTLING

Wilbur the Weak
vs.
Skinnyshanks

Heart-Condition Hal
vs.
The Kidney-Stone Kid

Legally Blind Larry
vs.
A. Stigmatic

Grandpa
vs.
Newborn Nate

ROZ CHAST

THREE-WAY MIRROR

FILES OF DOOM

ROZ CHAST

RATIONAL EXUBERANCE

My! This brisket is edible!

As of now, I'm not in chronic pain!

Whatever we're watching is not so bad that it makes me wish I'd never been born!

AFGHANIGAP

Classic

Cargo

Pleated Front

Flat Front

Slim fit with Lycra

Relaxed fit

Cropped

ROZ CHAST

NEW VOCABULARY WORDS FOR THE

NEWLY NON-MEGA-RICH

ROZ CHAST

ULTIMA THULE

By the time I was nine, I had a pretty good idea of where the borders of my neighborhood were.

COMPLETELY DIFFERENT SUBWAY LINE

STRANGE SMELLS

TOO MANY SEMI-DETACHED HOUSES

MARAUDERS AND HOODLUMS

THEY DON'T WANT YOU IN THEIR NEIGHBORHOOD, SO DON'T GO.

We rarely left it.

What's there that you can't get here?

Occasionally, we drove to a specific destination maybe fifteen minutes away.

Who wants to go to Kings Plaza?

I DO! I DO!

But we never explored, and we never lingered.

Could we just walk around?

No.

Could we stay for dinner?

No.

I don't know.

What would happen if we went all the way down to the end of that street?

That would have been pushing our luck.

What if we just went two blocks over?

When you grow up, you can go two blocks over.

And if somebody moved away—well, that was the end of them.

Whatever happened to the Krents?

They're in Canarsie now.

I thought about other neighborhoods in Brooklyn...

...like Red Hook, which was filled with drunken sailors, loose women, and stevedores...

BAR

DOGFIGHT

TATTOO

CONTENTS 500 LBS.

...Flatlands, which stretched flatly and unpopulatedly into oblivion...

...and Sea Gate, with its maze of Venetian canals, from which, once you entered, you'd never emerge...

All you had to do was go too far in the wrong direction, and off the edge of the earth you'd go.

I just wanted to see what was on the other side of McDonald Avenue!

R. Chast

ROZ CHAST

THE FIRST DAY BACK

NONMEDICAL·ALERT BRACELETS

ROZ CHAST

DREAM PARENTS

ROZ CHAST

THE RETURN OF MISS SUBWAYS

Millicent G.'s interests include cooking, table tennis, and avoiding eye contact whenever possible.

In addition to golf and poetry, Jan V. enjoys reading ads for torn-earlobe repair over and over again.

When not folk dancing or helping the needy, Hilda B. likes to think about the unlikelihood of tunnel collapse.

ROZ CHAST

THANK-YOU CARDS
FOR
RALPH NADER

Yosemite's a shopping mall,
The desert isn't there at all.
Alaska's an amusement park—
I guess you really made your mark.

Thanks a lot, jerk.

What is your problem?
Why did you run?
If it weren't for you,
Gore would have won.

Nice work, fella.

There's no doubt about it:
Your brain is first-rate.
Too bad that this wasn't
A high-school debate.

Hope you're happy now, twit.

When everyone can buy a gun
Without too much ado,
A few will say, "Who paved the way?"
And I will think of you.

Way to go, pal.

Once I was one of your ardent defenders—
If only you'd stuck with rating blenders.

You the man, Mr. N.

r. Chv

RECIPES FOR COMFORT DRINKS

Cozy

2 oz. hot cocoa
4 oz. vodka
3 marshmallows

Combine cocoa and vodka. Garnish with marshmallows. Serves one nicely, but it's your call.

The Healing Begins

2 tbsp. hot milk
1 tbsp. honey
4 oz. rum

Stir everything together. Should be fine for one, but if a tad more is needed, that's O.K.

Osama Who?

½ c. camomile tea
2 tsp. sugar
4 oz. Scotch

Mix tea, sugar, and Scotch. Makes one, but, hey, who are we to say?

Home Security

½ c. vanilla pudding
4 oz. gin

Blend pudding and gin. One ought to do the trick, but these are difficult times.

ROZ CHAST

HAUNTED NEW YORK

The Ghost Bus of 72nd Street

Goes back and forth but never, ever stops.

The Poltergeist of Bergdorf Goodman

Could there be any other explanation for why anyone would buy such a hideous garment?

The Accursed Storefront

One month, it's a gourmet cheese shop...then it's a karate studio... then a Czech restaurant...who will try their luck next?

The Ectoplasmic Super

People swear that they have seen him—but there is never any proof.

THEORIES OF EVERYTHING

ROZ CHAST

MY SPAM SKETCHBOOK:

Every time I check my e-mail, I get Spam from certain people. At first, their names sounded fairly believable. A "Mirella Borth" wanted to give me debt-consolidation tips. An "Alexander Clinebells" wondered if I would like a bigger penis, or maybe it was larger breasts. After a while, these names began to sound strange. They didn't sound at all like any names I'd ever heard before. They didn't sound like they came from any country on earth. Perhaps they came from Planet Spam...

Elba Rudd

Cleans office buildings in midtown.

Brasil ("rhymes with basil") Hinchcliff

Very snooty. Sells antiques.

Lacomb Ciliberto

Eurotrash, through and through.

Feodora Campeau

Lives in an apartment at Park and 61st with her dog, Zaza.

Biby Mulberry

Makes her own goat cheese in Vermont.

Carmen Glavin

Has been the bookkeeper for A-to-Z Imports, Inc., for nigh on forty years.

Ludwig Bialkenius

Math genius. Still working on dissertation at Columbia.

SECULAR CLOISTERS

FRED'S PRIORY

For menfolk only. Fishing, model railroads, football, gun talk, farm-machinery repair, etc. No women or woman talk allowed.

THE CONVENT OF BARBIE

A place where girls aged five through eleven can devote themselves to the study of Barbie, with no distractions from the outside world.

HEARTS SANCTUARY

Behind a sixty-foot-high wall, a quiet haven for men and women whose only wish is to play hearts from dawn till dusk.

CINEMA ABBEY

A shelter for people who have renounced everything in life except movies.

ROZ CHAST

ROZ CHAST

HOME ECONOMICS

LOW TIDE

TRANSLATION INTO
NON-CELEBRITESE

ENTERED REHAB

Went to Starbuck's; hid out with the paper for two hours.

HOSPITALIZED FOR EXHAUSTION

Took drool nap on sofa.

TAKING TIME OFF TO RE-EXAMINE PRIORITIES

Shopped for and purchased new dress, even though it was kind of expensive and not absolutely necessary.

ROZ CHAST

SUBURBAN LEGENDS

That weird, skeevy guy who's always picking through people's garbage is a Rockefeller scion.

Girls do "things" with boys on the high-school bus.

They're building a huge sewage-treatment plant behind the Food Baron.

Muffy's Golf Boutique sells whips and chains in the back.

Our town is owned by Bill Gates. He was passing through in '97 and thought it was "cool."

ALL TOO TRUE, UNFORTUNATELY

Viva Las

At Spring break, we go to Las Vegas.

DISNEYWORLD · LAS VEGAS

I always start these trips as the world's happiest camper.

This is going to be the BEST VACATION EVER!!!

Things go downhill pretty swiftly, though.

Why do you have that look on your face?

WHAT LOOK?

You could say I have money issues...

WHIRRRRRRRR. CLICK

INTERNAL CALCULATOR

...so maybe Vegas isn't the right place for me, but **anyway**...

SHEKELS FUGIUNT RESORT
DRINK 'N' BET
LOSE IT ALL
KISS-IT-ALL-GOODBYE
KASINO

In our hotel, there's a game arcade where the kids drop about fifty bucks a day.

We ran out of tokens!

WIN-O-MATIC · SLOTS O' FUN · MR. MONEY BAGS · CHANGE EATER · SKEE BALL

Sure, it's a lot, but they're **so** happy when they win something.

Look! I won a DOGGIE!

Dog = $43.50

Of course, now is not the time to get all chintzy about pay-per-view-in-hotel-room situations...

What do you want to watch next?

I dunno! This time, YOU pick!

...even when somebody accidentally sits on the remote and it has to be re-started,

Oops.

$9.95 + $9.95 + $9.95 + $9.95 + $9.95 + $9.95 + $9.95 + $9.95 + $9.95 + $9.95 + $9.95 + $9.95 + $9.95 + $9.95 + $9.95

or if people fall asleep after the movie's been on for only two minutes.

$9.95 + $9.95 + $9.95 + $9.95 + $9.95 + $9.95 + $9.95 + $9.95 + $9.95 + $9.95 + $9.95 + $9.95 + $9.95

So **what** if you're in a fancy restaurant and everyone is fighty?

Eww! frogs' legs! Why, that POOR LITTLE FROG!

SHUT UP, SHUT UP, SHUT UP!!! MOM!!!!!

Do you really think, on your deathbed, you'll miss that $287.19?

ROZ CHAST

Vegas

Uh-oh! All our clothes are dirty. Why not have the hotel do them?

I knew something was wrong when I saw the T-shirts all starched and pressed and hanging on a garment rack.

RAGE AGAINST THE MACHINE

That was sort of a low point.

SPROING!!!

$400

jeans
socks
T-shirts
ratty underwear

Oops- almost forgot the tip!

Here. Thank you.

At this point, Room Service barely registers.

Mom? Can we order banana splits?

And some fondue?

Sure, why not..

I have entered a SPENDING COMA.

After all, it's only money!

You can't take it with you!

In other words, I am ready to gamble.

POUR MONEY HERE 25¢

INCINERATOR CHUTE

JINGLE JANGLE

I throw away nearly a hundred quarters before I come to my senses.

JINGLE JANGLE

What the-

Where AM I ???

Quickly, I exchange the remainder for folding money.

PAI GOW

WHEW!

HANGE

At the airport, I try the slots one last time.

25¢ WILD CHERRY

POKER DOUBLE DIAMOND

Guess what happens?

YOU | LOSE | AGAIN
NOTHING | ZILCH | NADA
WHAT | A | SUCKER

25¢

Finally, we're in New York again, and back to reality.

Can I have a souvenir key chain?

BAGGAGE CLAIM →

GATES 3-7

NO *!G#ING WAY PAL!

THEORIES OF EVERYTHING

THE FATE THAT AWAITS US ALL

CREEPING ROONEYISM

THE LITTLE ENGINE THAT COULDA WOULDA SHOULDA

HOAX ETHNIC FOOD

ROZ CHAST

CHILDREN'S DREAM BEDTIME ROUTINE

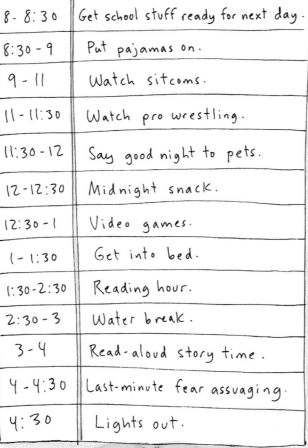

7:30 – 8	Brush teeth; wash hands and face.
8 – 8:30	Get school stuff ready for next day.
8:30 – 9	Put pajamas on.
9 – 11	Watch sitcoms.
11 – 11:30	Watch pro wrestling.
11:30 – 12	Say good night to pets.
12 – 12:30	Midnight snack.
12:30 – 1	Video games.
1 – 1:30	Get into bed.
1:30 – 2:30	Reading hour.
2:30 – 3	Water break.
3 – 4	Read-aloud story time.
4 – 4:30	Last-minute fear assuaging.
4:30	Lights out.

ROZ CHAST

SEASONAL AFFECTIVE DISORDERS
WINTER BLUES
BUS STOP
I HATE the cold... I HATE the ice... I HATE the filthy slush... I HATE this hat...
SPRING GUILT
It's 68° and PERFECT!
I should be outside, frolicking and gamboling... yet I don't like to frolic or gambol...
SUMMER MALAISE
Can't move... stuck to chair... very, very hot... brain melting... no air...
AUTUMN MELANCHOLY
And so, for no apparent reason, it all begins anew.

GROWN UP HAPPY MEALS

#1: Uncle Ed Special

Burger
Six gin-and-tonics
Lottery ticket
Aspirin

#2: Grandma's Delight

Burger
Bran muffin
Nineteen prunes
Metamucil shake

#3: New Ager

Burger
Herbal tea
Shiatsu foot massage
Scented candle
Windham Hill cassette

#4: Up, Up and Away

Burger
Seven coffees
Chocolate cake
Three cigarettes
Piece of nicotine gum
NoDoz

ROZ CHAST

NEW YEAR'S RESOLUTIONS
IN THE ANIMAL KINGDOM

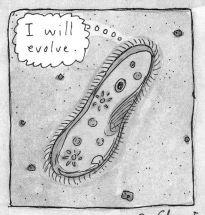

ROZ CHAST

Special Cards for Special Friends

Our kids are friends,
Yes, this is true -
But that doesn't mean
That we are, too.

~ Oh, well.

We've things in common
with each other,
But you remind me
of my mother.

~ It's such a shame.

You're never in a crappy mood,
You always buy organic food,
Your family is smart and nice,
You always give me good advice -
Yet every time that we converse,
I always feel a little worse.

~ Why IS that,
I wonder?

R. Chast

ROZ CHAST

TIRED OF BEING AN IDIOT? THEN CHECK OUT...

SUDDEN GENIUS~

AND START GETTING SMARTER TODAY!

#1036 - SmartSocks
These ultra-constrictive socks force the blood up into your brain. The pain means they're working.

$39.99

#2057 - The Einstein Diet
What _did_ this mega-genius eat? Read this book and unlock Albert's diet secrets.

$84.99

#3188 - Russian Headbox
Russian mystics have long known that putting one's head in a box concentrates the cranial aura.

- easy to use
- safe
- 100% effective

$124.99

#4590 - Neuron Aligner
Studies show that misaligned neurons may lead to impaired brain functionality.

BEFORE   AFTER

$267.99

#6856 - I.Q. Patches
Each patch contains one I.Q. point. Go to bed stupid- wake up a **GENIUS!**

$599.99 per dozen

R. Chr

VIVE LA RÉSISTANCE

ROZ CHAST

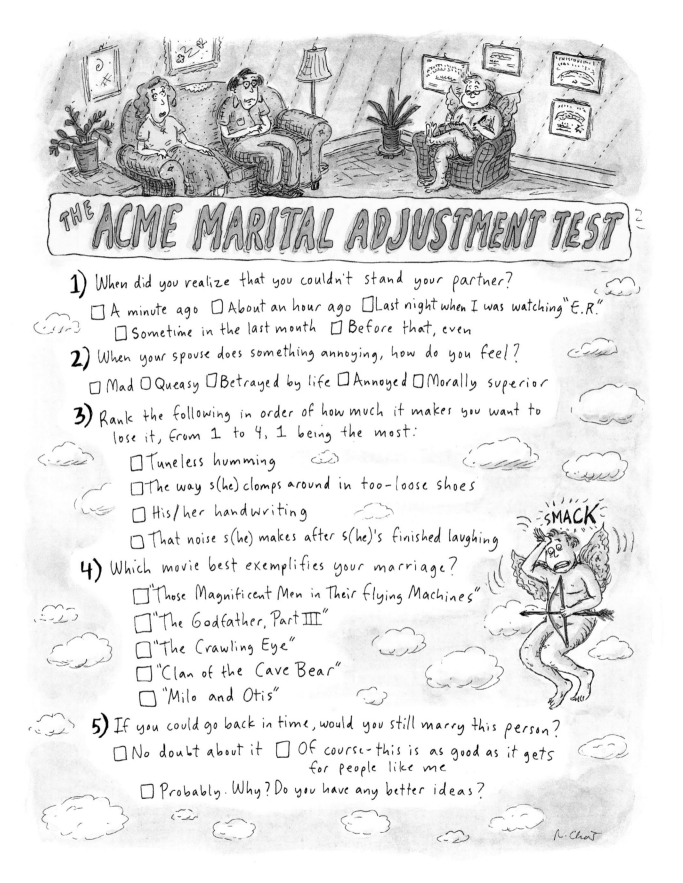

THE ACME MARITAL ADJUSTMENT TEST

1) When did you realize that you couldn't stand your partner?

☐ A minute ago ☐ About an hour ago ☐ Last night when I was watching "E.R."
☐ Sometime in the last month ☐ Before that, even

2) When your spouse does something annoying, how do you feel?

☐ Mad ☐ Queasy ☐ Betrayed by life ☐ Annoyed ☐ Morally superior

3) Rank the following in order of how much it makes you want to lose it, from 1 to 4, 1 being the most:

☐ Tuneless humming
☐ The way s(he) clomps around in too-loose shoes
☐ His/her handwriting
☐ That noise s(he) makes after s(he)'s finished laughing

4) Which movie best exemplifies your marriage?

☐ "Those Magnificent Men in Their Flying Machines"
☐ "The Godfather, Part III"
☐ "The Crawling Eye"
☐ "Clan of the Cave Bear"
☐ "Milo and Otis"

5) If you could go back in time, would you still marry this person?

☐ No doubt about it ☐ Of course—this is as good as it gets for people like me
☐ Probably. Why? Do you have any better ideas?

SMACK

R. Chast

BUSH'S FOREIGN POLICIES

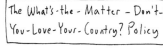

The Leave-War-to-the-Professionals-and-Don't-Bother-Your-Pretty-Little-Head-About-It Policy

The What's-the-Matter-Don't-You-Love-Your-Country? Policy

The Here's-Fifty-Bucks-Now-Go-to-the-Mall-and-Quit-Bugging-Me Policy

R. Chast

CHEERLEADERS FROM ANOTHER PLANET

ROZ CHAST

NEWEST ITEMS FROM THE COOLER IMAGE

THE CATALOGUE FOR BOYS WITH A THIRTEEN-YEAR-OLD BODY AND A ZERO-YEAR-OLD BRAIN!

#1039- Jet-Pack T-shirt

Oh, man - this is SO GREAT! All you do is pull the cord and you'll fly hundreds of feet up in the sky!

WHOOO-EEE!!!!

#1178 - Connect-O-Cord

Now you can hook up the toaster, the air-conditioner, your dad's computer, the microwave, and a foot massager. Why? Because it's **COOL.**

#2034-All-Time-Great Bully Taunts

Admit it: there is nothing like riling up the biggest, meanest, dumbest kid on the block.

#3616- Exploding Pencil

"But is it worth a two-week suspension?" **NEED YOU ASK?!?!?**

#5042-Tiki-Torch Trampoline

You can really get messed up on one of these! UH-OH!! **MOM!!!!!!**

R-Clv

THEORIES OF EVERYTHING

SMOKING PORN

TOBACCO ORGY

Behind closed doors, it's a swingin', puffin', ashtray-strewn, lightin'-up, inhalin' world.

FORBIDDEN DELIGHT

Milt's vice is totally secret— until a co-worker makes an "interesting" discovery!

NATIONAL SMOKE-O-GRAPHIC

Curious and unusual smoking practices from around the globe.

WALK
WHY BOTHER?

introducing ROACH-HAB.

ROACH PRISON

Roaches check in, but they don't check out until they've paid their debt to society.

SPA DE ROACH

Roaches check in, but they don't check out until they've gotten back in touch with themselves.

ROACH UNIVERSITY

Roaches check in, but they don't check out until they've learned some real-life skills.

ROZ CHAST

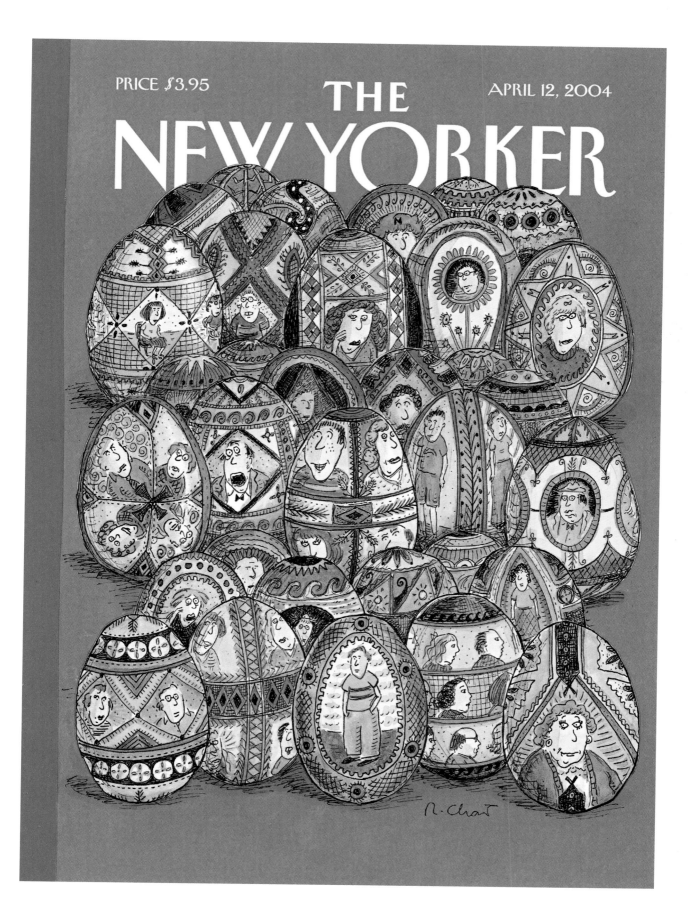

PRICE $3.95

THE NEW YORKER

APRIL 12, 2004

ROZ CHAST

ADULT ATTENTION DEFICIT DISORDERS
(A.A.D.D.)

Financial Information Disorder (F.I.D.)

You like money and wish you had more of it. But the minute you hear "capital-gains tax" your eyeballs roll back in your head.

Technical Manual Fatigue Syndrome (T.M.F.S.)

Finally, an explanation as to why a bright fellow like you can't program your VCR.

Driving Directions Deafness (D.D.D.)

This Good Samaritan might as well be talking to that parking meter over there.

Other People Non-Attention Condition (O.P.N.A.C.)

If it's not about you, forget it.

ROZ CHAST

Poetry Corner

JUNIOR HIGH EDITION

THEORIES OF EVERYTHING

ROZ CHAST

THOMAS PYNCHON'S EVIL TWIN

Mud-wrestle in my underwear on national TV while holding up a copy of my new book? NO PROBLEMO!

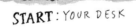

NAPQUEST

START: YOUR DESK
FINISH: LIVING-ROOM SOFA
EST. DISTANCE: .00008 MILE
EST. TIME: 7.5 SECONDS

① At the end of your chair, make a right.	.00001 mile
② Continue till end of desk and make a sharp left.	.00001 mile
③ Go straight on carpet.	.00003 mile
④ Bear left at end of carpet.	.00002 mile
⑤ Turn left onto sofa.	.00001 mile

ROZ CHAST

REGRETS *only*

Sometimes, when one thinks about one's ancestors, one can become sort of incredibly furious. 	For instance, here is a nice house right on the ocean. It costs $5.5 million. 	10 years ago, it was $2.5 million. 20 years ago, it was one million.  *Even so…* *Oh, well…*
But 200 years ago it was $1,000 - *if that!* *Say!*	Where were one's ancestors when land was still affordable? 	Probably sitting around in some back-water country, twiddling their lazy thumbs… TWIDDLE TWIDDLE TWIDDLE 
…or arguing about whether somebody did or did not get rooked at the chicken store. 	It can make a person **ILL** to think about this. 	Some ancestors understood things. *I'll have 20 acres of oceanfront… …and make it SNAPPY!* 
But other ancestors were too busy KNITTING SHAWLS. 	"Can't come to the U.S. and buy property - I have to finish SCRUBBING THIS TEAKETTLE!" *There's nothing like a clean tea-kettle!* 	Such self-centeredness is appalling. *This teakettle belonged to your great-great-great-grandmother!* *Gee.* 

R.C.T

ROZ CHAST

SON OF
HOWL

WITH APOLOGIES TO ALLEN GINSBERG

I saw the best minds of my generation

destroyed by madness.

If you don't bring up your board scores, you might as well just FORGET YOUR LIFE!

starving, hysterical, naked,

Who says? I'm PERFECT!

dragging themselves through Stop'n'Shop at dawn looking for low-fat Triscuits...

These aren't LOW-FAT... they're LOW-SALT!

Yukon Gold potatoes...

They have to be YUKON GOLD. They can't just be IDAHO.

and nam pla.

WHERE are they HIDING the NAM PLA???...

R.Chast

THEORIES OF EVERYTHING

ROZ CHAST

THE SPECIALS

Comes the Revolution FAIRY TALES

When peasants find out who the princess is by using the old mattress-pea trick, they kill her.

Cinderella's stepmother, her stepsisters, and Prince Charming are all killed in an uprising as Cinderella runs off with Henri, an idealistic student.

The Frog Prince realizes that he's just lucky to be alive.

ROZ CHAST

The New York Review of Weather
TABLE OF CONTENTS
YOU CALL THIS SPRING?
by Joe Metatarsal
~page 3
THIS ISN'T COLD—
I'LL SHOW YOU COLD!
by Wanda Vem III
~page 6
I HATE HOW WANDA CAN BE SUCH A WEATHER BULLY
by Sheena Crickettes
~page 11
ISN'T IT NEAT, OR AT LEAST SOMEWHAT INTERESTING, THAT PEOPLE CAN PERCEIVE WEATHER SO DIFFERENTLY?
by Marty McPincus
~page 13
MARTY, SHUT YER YAPPER!
by Ed Fennimore-Lattimore
~page 16
SPRING: THE OVERRATED SEASON
by "Birdie" Wilkins
~page 20
R. Chast

ROZ CHAST

ROZ CHAST

PHYSICS: THE FINAL EXAM

At dinner, Andy keeps leaning back in his chair. At what angle will he fall over?

What is the fastest speed of rotation which can be attained before someone flies into space?

According to the Pythagorean Theory of Spillage, how long can a Slurpee and a laptop be adjacent to one another before disaster occurs?

Is it possible to pour a one-gallon bottle of orange soda into a twelve-ounce thermos? Why or why not?

Based on Laws of Melto-Dynamics, at what time will everything in the refrigerator below be spoiled if it is now 11 A.M.?

Explain the circumstances under which matter can, and probably WILL disappear from the Universe.

RECOMMENDED TESTS for ages 21+

ANNUAL DECREP-OGRAM
A simple X-ray which tells your doctor just how fast everything is deteriorating.

BIANNUAL DECREP-ONOSCOPY
What's brewing deep, deep inside? Anything "interesting"? Let's have a look-see.

ONCE-EVERY-FIVE-YEARS FULL-BODY 'CREP SCAN
Put an end to idle musing about what's decrepit and what's not.

ANOTHER DAY IN THE SALT MINES

ROZ CHAST

LIMITED EDITION CARDS

TO: Harry Whittington
FROM: Dick Cheney

GET WELL AS FAST AS YOU POSSIBLY CAN

SORRY FOR ACCIDENTALLY SHOOTING YOU IN THE FACE

THANK YOU FOR NOT DYING

YOUR NAME NOT HERE!

You really gave me quite
a start,
You really made me worry,
So I say with all my heart,
Relax and heal — and hurry.

~ Someone who
cares deeply
about you.

When all this is over,
When all this ends,
Here is hoping
We'll still be friends.

~ I owe you
BIG TIME.

Violets are blue,
Lilies are white,
Whatever you do,
Stay away from "the light."

~ Don't act like you
don't know what
I'm talking about.

R. Chast

ROZ CHAST

FORGET PARIS! FORGET VENICE! FORGET NEW YORK! THIS YEAR, TRY

THE VINEYARDIA-

LAS VEGAS'S [NEW] MARTHA'S VINEYARD-THEMED HOTEL!

- ⚙ AUTHENTIC-LOOKING SHINGLED ROOF!
- ⚙ SEAGULL-AND-WAVE SURROUND SOUND!
- ⚙ VINTAGE TV SET IN EVERY ROOM!
- ⚙ COMPLIMENTARY PRE-1980s PAPERBACKS!
- ⚙ MILDEWY SMELL THROUGHOUT!
- ⚙ DOZENS OF "LOCAL CHARACTERS" PROVIDED FOR YOUR ENTERTAINMENT! (NUTTY OLD HEIRESS, CRUSTY FISHERMAN, BITTER EX-FAMOUS WRITER, ETC.)
- ⚙ WALK ON OUR "BEACH" AND LOOK FOR "SHELLS"!
- ⚙ VIRTUAL BODYSURFING AND BIKE RIDING!

VISIT OUR WEB SITE FOR A COMPLETE LIST OF ATTRACTIONS www.lasvegasvineyardia.com

R. Chast

MAIL-ORDER MOMS

Want a mom who'll let you stay up as late as you want? Who'll let you watch anything on TV? I'm waiting. Box 7291.

Like candy and cake? Hate green vegetables? Then I'm the mom for you. Box 2805.

I'll stay home and play games with you __all day long__: Donkey Kong, rummy, whatever. No "life of my own" for me! I'm here- where are you? Box 6433.

No rules, anything goes. After all, it's _your_ life. Just say the word and I'm yours. Box 4116.

R. Chst

INTRODUCING *Honest Abe* CARDS

There comes a time in life
when a truth -
however painful -
must be faced.

So,
with boundless love,
let me say this:

You should brush
your teeth
more often.

Existence
Is a mystery.
No one has the answers.
Nothing is for certain -
Except one thing:
Everyone hates your laugh.

Like two rocks on the beach,
You and I sit for eternity.
I just wanted to tell you how
BEAUTIFUL
you are ~
Except for that thing on your chin.

ROZ CHAST

R. Chast

ROZ CHAST

FIRST-PERIOD ALGEBRA

MARILYN MANQUÉ

All-Verbal Westerns

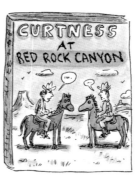

PRESCRIPTION AIR FRESHENERS

A no-nonsense freshener that takes care of just about any problem.

Light yet effective: perfect for everyday use.

When you don't want to fool around, reach for the Meadow.

ALL OF MY HOPES AND DREAMS, CRUSHED, SERVED ON A BUN (WITH MUSTARD)

AS YET TO BE PROVEN

DALYRIMPLE'S CONJECTURE

If I say it makes sense to drive forty miles to save three cents a gallon on gasoline, it makes sense.

JUDY SUE'S PROJECTION

Whatever is in *THIS BOWL* will fit into *THAT TUPPERWARE CONTAINER*.

MARVIN'S CALCULATION

With every container of **no**-fat, plain yogurt I consume, I increase my lifespan by fifteen minutes.

BETTY'S THEOREM

It doesn't matter if something I buy turns out to be a mistake and unreturnable, because seven years ago, I found eighty dollars on the street, so *that balances everything out*.

ROZ CHAST

My Dream House

I wouldn't mind having a little townhouse on a pretty, tree-lined street in Manhattan.

It should have a nice, normal kitchen and a dining room. No twelve-burner stove or massive refrigerator.

A few guest bedrooms would be nice for when my favorite friends are visiting.

I'd like lots of separate art studios. The main one would be for drawing cartoons.

But there would be several others, for passing enthusiasms.

I'd like a library...
You have so many wonderful books about salt!

and a room for watching movies and TV shows...
Tonight we're seeing "Sunset Boulevard"!
It's a REAL CLASSIC!

My bedroom would contain a stairway leading up to a rooftop observatory, which I would learn how to use

And here and there, I'd like a room that served no purpose at all - it would be just "extra."
Pull up a chair!

I don't want an all-white Zen retreat or a Southwestern Special or anything too old or too new! And none of those bathrooms that take you 15 minutes to figure out how the faucets work!! And no room full of Nautilus machines!!!

...although a little pool in my backyard would be delightful. Nothing fancy.

IS THAT TOO MUCH TO ASK?

THEORIES OF EVERYTHING

ROZ CHAST

Other People

Other people have at least one glamorous relative.

Other people do not have a secret symptom that they worry about.

Other people lead complicated, rich, secretive personal lives.

Other people are not enraged by jars of dried pasta used as décor.

Other people know how they want their living rooms to look.

Other people know exactly what the Federal Reserve is.

ROZ CHAST

A NOTE ON THE TYPE